The Gig Book

Bob Dylan

Published by
Wise Publications
14-15 Berners Street,
London W1T 3LJ, UK.

Exclusive Distributors:
Music Sales Limited
Distribution Centre,
Newmarket Road, Bury St Edmunds,
Suffolk IP33 3YB, UK.
Music Sales Pty Limited
20 Resolution Drive, Caringbah,
NSW 2229, Australia.

Order No. AM997304
ISBN 978-1-84938-071-3

Compiled by Nick Crispin.
Text by Graham Vickers.
Picture research by Jacqui Black.
Photographs courtesy of Gettyimages except
pages 25 and 89 (Redferns), page 217
(Corbis) and page 263 (© Danny Clinch).
Music engraved by Paul Ewers Music Design.
Edited by Tom Farncombe
and Adrian Hopkins.
Design by Fresh Lemon.

www.musicsales.com

Printed in China by PWGS/MRM Graphics Ltd.

Your Guarantee of Quality:
As publishers, we strive to produce every
book to the highest commercial standards.

The music has been freshly engraved and
the book has been carefully designed to
minimise awkward page turns and to make
playing from it a real pleasure.

Particular care has been given to specifying
acid-free, neutral-sized paper made from
pulps which have not been elemental chlorine
bleached.

This pulp is from farmed sustainable forests
and was produced with special regard for the
environment.

Throughout, the printing and binding
have been planned to ensure a sturdy,
attractive publication which should give
years of enjoyment.

If your copy fails to meet our high standards,
please inform us and we will gladly replace it.

Wise Publications
part of **The Music Sales Group**
London / New York / Paris / Sydney / Copenhagen / Berlin / Tokyo / Madrid

The GigBook Bob Dylan

Introduction

This new Bob Dylan GigBook takes songs from a long career that started in New York's Greenwich Village of the early 60s and then went off in many forward-looking musical directions over the next half-century. Anyone expecting a predominantly acoustic-period Dylan collection of songs may be pleasantly surprised by the sheer musical variety of the material presented here.

From the plaintive 1983 song 'Blind Willie McTell' (recorded with Mark Knopfler and held back from release until 1991) to the hypnotic 'Not Dark Yet' from *Time Out of Mind*, every number reminds us that Dylan's music has spanned generations. Musical fashion comes and goes, but Dylan has made timeless music for almost five decades. He's also a great scholar of different musical genres, and so there is plenty of scope to try out different styles of playing and singing here. 'Hurricane' is an angry broadside reminiscent of Dylan's earliest songs about social injustice. 'Romance in Durango'—from a classic 1970s album, *Desire*—just oozes Mexican atmosphere while 'Brownsville Girl'

(the result of a songwriting collaboration with playwright Sam Shepard) runs for more than eleven minutes and its lyric even contains a précis of *The Gunfighter*, a 1950 Gregory Peck movie, surely making it a genre-defying song.

If you're not ready for the challenge of some of Dylan's more epic numbers ('Isis' is another heroic narrative ballad) then you'll still be able to find plenty of simpler, shorter songs to perform from this unique singer-songwriter's output, a catalogue that forms one of the major strands of modern popular music.

Play! Enjoy! Don't look back...

100
DYLAN
SONGS

New Kid On The Block

Before he became an influential figure himself, Bob Dylan was very much under the influence of others. His early love of 50s pop would only become well-known in later years but Buddy Holly and Little Richard were his early heroes, soon to be displaced by Woody Guthrie. Dylan's first album, *Bob Dylan* (1962), contained only two original compositions. It was Dylan's first step in what was to be a long, shape-shifting career. One album later *The Freewheelin' Bob Dylan* (1963) saw Dylan's own voice starting to emerge in a clutch of self-penned songs that included 'Blowin' In The Wind', 'A Hard Rain's A-Gonna Fall' and 'Don't Think Twice, It's All Right'. Those two political broadsides and a rueful love song indicated where the young folkie was headed. 'Tomorrow Is A Long Time', also included here, was a song from the same time that never made it to a non-bootleg album until many years later.

Blowin' In The Wind

Words & Music by Bob Dylan

Moderately

Capo fret 7

1. How many roads must a man walk down Be-
(Verses 2 & 3 see block lyrics)

-fore you call him a man? Yes, 'n'

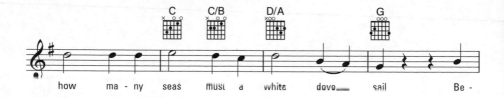

how many seas must a white dove sail Be-

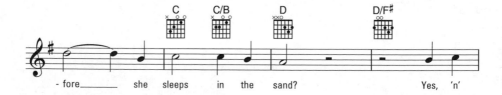

-fore she sleeps in the sand? Yes, 'n'

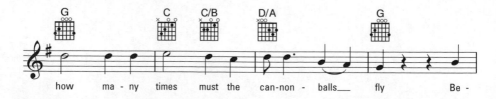

how many times must the can-non-balls fly Be-

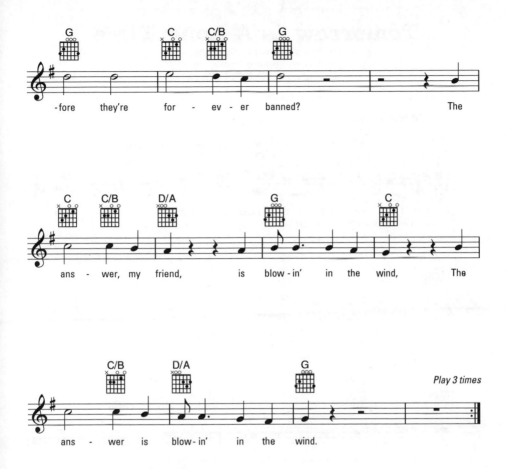

G   C   C/B   G

-fore   they're   for   -   ev   -   er   banned?   The

C   C/B   D/A   G   C

ans - wer,   my   friend,   is   blow - in'   in   the   wind,   The

C/B   D/A   G   *Play 3 times*

ans -   wer   is   blow - in'   in   the   wind.

Verse 2:
How many years can a mountain exist
Before it's washed to the sea?
Yes, 'n' how many years can some people exist
Before they're allowed to be free?
Yes, 'n' how many times can a man turn his head
Pretending he just doesn't see?
The answer, my friend, is blowin' in the wind
The answer is blowin' in the wind

Verse 3:
How many times must a man look up
Before he can see the sky?
Yes, 'n' how many ears must one man have
Before he can hear people cry?
Yes, 'n' how many deaths will it take till he knows
That too many people have died?
The answer, my friend, is blowin' in the wind
The answer is blowin' in the wind

9

Tomorrow Is A Long Time

Words & Music by Bob Dylan

1. If to - day was not an end-less high-way, If to -
(Verses 2 & 3 see block lyrics)

- night was not a crook-ed trail, If to -

- mor - row was-n't such a long time, Then

lone - some-would mean no-thing to you at all. Yes, and

Chorus

on - ly if my own true love was wait - in' Yes, and if

10

I could hear her heart a - soft - ly pound - in',_____

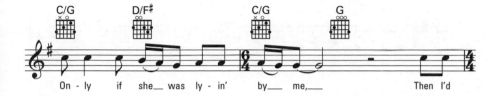

On - ly if she__ was ly - in' by__ me,__ Then I'd

Play 3 times

lie in my bed_____ once__ a - gain. 2. I can't

Verse 2:
I can't see my reflection in the waters
I can't speak the sounds that show no pain
I can't hear the echo of my footsteps
Or can't remember the sound of my own name
Chorus:

Verse 3:
There's beauty in the silver, singin' river
There's beauty in the sunrise in the sky
But none of these and nothing else can touch the beauty
That I remember in my true love's eyes
Chorus:

Ballad Of Hollis Brown

Words & Music by Bob Dylan

To match original recording, tune down one semitone

Moderately

Hol-lis Brown, He lived on the out-side of town, Hol-lis

Brown, He lived on the out-side of town, With his

wife and five child-ren And his cab-in fall-in' down.

Verse

1. You looked for work and mon-ey And you walked a rug-ged mile,___
(Verses 2-10 see block lyrics)

You looked for work and mon-ey And you walked a rug-ged mile.___

Your child-ren are so hun-gry That they

1-9.   **10.**

don't know how to smile.___   2. Your

12

Verse 2:
Your baby's eyes look crazy
They're a-tuggin' at your sleeve
Your baby's eyes look crazy
They're a-tuggin' at your sleeve
You walk the floor and wonder why
With every breath you breathe

Verse 3:
The rats have got your flour
Bad blood it got your mare
The rats have got your flour
Bad blood it got your mare
If there's anyone that knows
Is there anyone that cares?

Verse 4:
You prayed to the Lord above
Oh please send you a friend
You prayed to the Lord above
Oh please send you a friend
Your empty pockets tell yuh
That you ain't a-got no friend

Verse 5:
Your babies are crying louder
It's pounding on your brain
Your babies are crying louder now
It's pounding on your brain
Your wife's screams are stabbin' you
Like the dirty drivin' rain

Verse 6:
Your grass it is turning black
There's no water in your well
Your grass is turning black
There's no water in your well
You spent your last lone dollar
On seven shotgun shells

Verse 7:
Way out in the wilderness
A cold coyote calls
Way out in the wilderness
A cold coyote calls
Your eyes fix on the shotgun
That's hangin' on the wall

Verse 8:
Your brain is a-bleedin'
And your legs can't seem to stand
Your brain is a-bleedin'
And your legs can't seem to stand
Your eyes fix on the shotgun
That you're holdin' in your hand

Verse 9:
There's seven breezes a-blowin'
All around the cabin door
There's seven breezes a-blowin'
All around the cabin door
Seven shots ring out
Like the ocean's pounding roar

Verse 10:
There's seven people dead
On a South Dakota farm
There's seven people dead
On a South Dakota farm
Somewhere in the distance
There's seven new people born

13

A Hard Rain's A-Gonna Fall

Words & Music by Bob Dylan

Moderately

Capo fret 2

1. Oh, where have you been, my blue-eyed son? Oh, where have you

(Verses 2-5 see block lyrics)

been, my dar-ling young one? I've

stum-bled on the side of__ twelve mist-y moun-tains, I've

walked and I've crawled on__ six crook-ed high-ways, I've

stepped in the mid-dle of__ sev-en sad for-ests, I've

been out in front of a do-zen dead o-ceans.

I've been

ten thou-sand miles in the mouth of a grave-yard,

And it's a

hard, and it's a hard, it's a hard, and it's a

hard, and it's a hard rain's

a-gon-na fall.

Play 5 times

2. Oh,

Verse 2:
Oh, what did you see, my blue-eyed son?
Oh, what did you see, my darling young one?
I saw a newborn baby with wild wolves all around it
I saw a highway of diamonds with nobody on it
I saw a black branch with blood that kept drippin'
I saw a room full of men with their hammers a-bleedin'
I saw a white ladder all covered with water
I saw ten thousand talkers whose tongues were all broken
I saw guns and sharp swords in the hands of young children
And it's a hard, and it's a hard, it's a hard, it's a hard
And it's a hard rain's a-gonna fall

Verse 3:
And what did you hear, my blue-eyed son?
And what did you hear, my darling young one?
I heard the sound of a thunder, it roared out a warnin'
Heard the roar of a wave that could drown the whole world
Heard one hundred drummers whose hands were a-blazin'
Heard ten thousand whisperin' and nobody listenin'
Heard one person starve, I heard many people laughin'
Heard the song of a poet who died in the gutter
Heard the sound of a clown who cried in the alley
And it's a hard, and it's a hard, it's a hard, it's a hard
And it's a hard rain's a-gonna fall

Verse 4:
Oh, who did you meet, my blue-eyed son?
Who did you meet, my darling young one?
I met a young child beside a dead pony
I met a white man who walked a black dog
I met a young woman whose body was burning
I met a young girl, she gave me a rainbow
I met one man who was wounded in love
I met another man who was wounded with hatred
And it's a hard, it's a hard, it's a hard, it's a hard
It's a hard rain's a-gonna fall

Verse 5:
Oh, what'll you do now, my blue-eyed son?
Oh, what'll you do now, my darling young one?
I'm a-goin' back out 'fore the rain starts a fallin'
I'll walk to the depths of the deepest black forest
Where the people are many and their hands are all empty
Where the pellets of poison are flooding their waters
Where the home in the valley meets the damp dirty prison
Where the executioner's face is always well hidden
Where hunger is ugly, where souls are forgotten
Where black is the color, where none is the number
And I'll tell it and think it and speak it and breathe it
And reflect it from the mountain so all souls can see it
Then I'll stand on the ocean until I start sinkin'
But I'll know my song well before I start singin'
And it's a hard, it's a hard, it's a hard, it's a hard
It's a hard rain's a-gonna fall

Don't Think Twice, It's All Right

Words & Music by Bob Dylan

Moderately

Capo fret 4

1. It ain't no use___ to sit and won-der why, babe

(Verse 2 see block lyrics)

It don't mat - ter, a - ny - how. An' it

ain't no use___ to sit and won-der why, babe___

If you don't know by now. When your

roost - er crows at the break of dawn Look out your

win - dow and_____ I'll be gone You're the

rea - son I'm trav' - lin'   on   Don't think twice, it's all

1.

2.

right.   2. It   right.   3. It

ain't no use___ in call - in'   out my name, gal___
(Verse 4 see block lyrics)

Like   you   nev - er   did   be - fore.   It

ain't no use___ in call - in'   out my name, gal___

I   can't hear you an - y   more.   I'm a -

- think - in' and a - won - d'rin' all the   way   down the road   I

once loved a wo - man, a child I'm told I

give her my heart but she want-ed my soul But don't think

1.
twice, It's all right.

2.
4. I'm right.

Verse 2:
It ain't no use in turnin' on your light, babe
That light I never knowed
An' it ain't no use in turnin' on your light, babe
I'm on the dark side of the road
Still I wish there was somethin' you would do or say
To try and make me change my mind and stay
We never did too much talkin' anyway
So don't think twice, it's all right

Verse 4:
I'm walkin' down that long, lonesome road, babe
Where I'm bound, I can't tell
But goodbye's too good a word, gal
So I'll just say fare thee well
I ain't sayin' you treated me unkind
You could have done better but I don't mind
You just kinda wasted my precious time
But don't think twice, it's all right

19

Masters Of War

Words & Music by Bob Dylan

Moderately

Capo fret 3

1. Come you mas - ters of war
(Verses 2-8 see block lyrics)
You that build all the guns

You that build the death planes

You that build the big bombs

You that hide be-hind walls

You that hide be-hind desks

I just want you to know I can see through your masks.

Play 8 times

2. You that

20

Verse 2:
You that never done nothin'
But build to destroy
You play with my world
Like it's your little toy
You put a gun in my hand
And you hide from my eyes
And you turn and run farther
When the fast bullets fly

Verse 3:
Like Judas of old
You lie and deceive
A world war can be won
You want me to believe
But I see through your eyes
And I see through your brain
Like I see through the water
That runs down my drain

Verse 4:
You fasten the triggers
For the others to fire
Then you set back and watch
When the death count gets higher
You hide in your mansion
As young people's blood
Flows out of their bodies
And is buried in the mud

Verse 5:
You've thrown the worst fear
That can ever be hurled
Fear to bring children
Into the world
For threatening my baby
Unborn and unnamed
You ain't worth the blood
That runs in your veins

Verse 6:
How much do I know
To talk out of turn
You might say that I'm young
You might say I'm unlearned
But there's one thing I know
Though I'm younger than you
Even Jesus would never
Forgive what you do

Verse 7:
Let me ask you one question
Is your money that good
Will it buy you forgiveness
Do you think that it could
I think you will find
When your death takes its toll
All the money you made
Will never buy back your soul

Verse 8:
And I hope that you die
And your death'll come soon
I will follow your casket
In the pale afternoon
And I'll watch as you're lowered
Down to your deathbed
And I'll stand o'er your grave
'Til I'm sure that you're dead

Girl From The North Country

Words & Music by Bob Dylan

Moderately

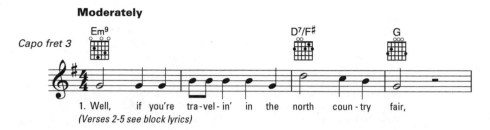

1. Well, if you're tra-vel-in' in the north coun-try fair,
(Verses 2-5 see block lyrics)

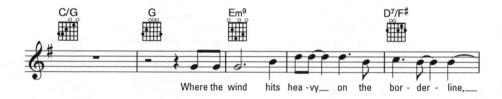

Where the wind hits hea-vy__ on the bor-der-line,__

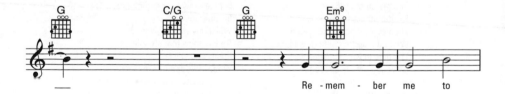

Re-mem-ber me to

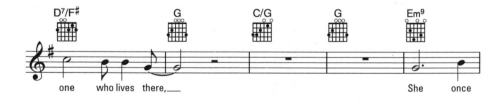

one who lives there,__ She once

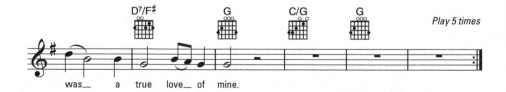

was__ a true love__ of mine.

Play 5 times

22

Verse 2:
Well, if you go when the snowflakes storm
When the rivers freeze and summer ends
Please see if she's wearing a coat so warm
To keep her from the howlin' winds

Verse 3:
Please see for me if her hair hangs long
If it rolls and flows all down her breast
Please see for me if her hair hangs long
That's the way I remember her best

Verse 4:
I'm a-wonderin' if she remembers me at all
Many times I've often prayed
In the darkness of my night
In the brightness of my day

Verse 5:
So if you're travelin' in the north country fair
Where the winds hit heavy on the borderline
Remember me to one who lives there
She once was a true love of mine

Songs Of Social Conscience

By the time of Dylan's third album, *The Times They Are A-Changin'* (1964), he was recording only his own compositions, many of them focusing on social and political change. Grimmer and sparer, this album cemented Dylan's reputation as a serious social commentator, mainly because of its 'true' story songs like 'Only A Pawn In Their Game' and 'Ballad Of Hollis Brown'. *Another Side of Bob Dylan* came out in the same year and marked a move away from his folk-politico stance towards songs with deeper poetic focus, which he still performed as a lone acoustic troubadour. It was an influential track listing. 'My Back Pages' was covered by The Byrds, Johnny Cash took a rockabilly stab at 'It Ain't Me Babe' and the bitter-sweet 'To Ramona' became a folk circuit favourite. The scene was now set for the big Dylan sea change of going electric.

With God On Our Side

Words & Music by Bob Dylan

Moderately, with freedom

1. Oh, my name it is no - thin'_____ My age it means

(Verses 2-9 see block lyrics)

less, The coun - try I come

from_____ Is called the Mid - west. I's

taught and brought up there The laws to a -

- bide And that land that I live

in Has God on its side.

Play 9 times

2. Oh the

26

Verse 2:
Oh the history books tell it
They tell it so well
The cavalries charged
The Indians fell
The cavalries charged
The Indians died
Oh the country was young
With God on its side

Verse 3:
Oh the Spanish-American
War had its day
And the Civil War too
Was soon laid away
And the names of the heroes
I's made to memorize
With guns in their hands
And God on their side

Verse 4:
Oh the First World War, boys
It closed out its fate
The reason for fighting
I never got straight
But I learned to accept it
Accept it with pride
For you don't count the dead
When God's on your side

Verse 5:
When the Second World War
Came to an end
We forgave the Germans
And we were friends
Though they murdered six million
In the ovens they fried
The Germans now too
Have God on their side

Verse 6:
I've learned to hate Russians
All through my whole life
If another war starts
It's them we must fight
To hate them and fear them
To run and to hide
And accept it all bravely
With God on my side

Verse 7:
But now we got weapons
Of the chemical dust
If fire them we're forced to
Then fire them we must
One push of the button
And a shot the world wide
And you never ask questions
When God's on your side

Verse 8:
Through many dark hour
I've been thinkin' about this
That Jesus Christ
Was betrayed by a kiss
But I can't think for you
You'll have to decide
Whether Judas Iscariot
Had God on his side

Verse 9:
So now as I'm leavin'
I'm weary as Hell
The confusion I'm feelin'
Ain't no tongue can tell
The words fill my head
And fall to the floor
If God's on our side
He'll stop the next war

Only A Pawn In Their Game

Words & Music by Bob Dylan

Freely

Capo fret 2

1. A bul - let from the back of a bush took

Med - gar Ev - ers' blood. A fin - ger

fired the trig - ger to his name. A han - dle hid

out in the dark, A hand set the spark, Two

eyes took the aim_____ Be -
-hind a man's brain_____ But
he can't be blamed_____ He's on - ly a

pawn in their game._____

2. A South pol - i - tic - ian prea-ches to the poor white
(Verses 3-5 see block lyrics)

man, "You got more than the

blacks, don't com - plain. You're bet-ter than them,___ you been

born with white skin," they ex - plain And the

Ne - gro's name Is used it is plain For the
pol - i - tic - ian's gain As he ri - ses to fame And the
poor white re - mains On the ca - boose of the train But it

Play 3 times
(D.S.)

ain't him to blame He's on - ly a pawn in their game.___

29

Verse 3:
The deputy sheriffs, the soldiers, the governors get paid
And the marshals and cops get the same
But the poor white man's used in the hands of them all like a tool
He's taught in his school
From the start by the rule
That the laws are with him
To protect his white skin
To keep up his hate
So he never thinks straight
'Bout the shape that he's in
But it ain't him to blame
He's only a pawn in their game

Verse 4:
From the poverty shacks, he looks from the cracks to the tracks
And the hoofbeats pound in his brain
And he's taught how to walk in a pack
Shoot in the back
With his fist in a clinch
To hang and to lynch
To hide 'neath the hood
To kill with no pain
Like a dog on a chain
He ain't got no name
But it ain't him to blame
He's only a pawn in their game

Verse 5:
Today, Medgar Evers was buried from the bullet he caught
They lowered him down as a king
But when the shadowy sun sets on the one
That fired the gun
He'll see by his grave
On the stone that remains
Carved next to his name
His epitaph plain:
Only a pawn in their game

Chimes Of Freedom

Words & Music by Bob Dylan

chimes of free-dom flash-ing

Flash-ing for the war-ri-ors whose strength is

not to fight, Flash-ing for the re-fu-gees___

___ on the un-armed road of flight An' for

each an' ev-'ry un-der-dog sol-dier

in the night___ An' we gazed up-on the chimes of

Play 6 times

free-dom flash-ing.

2. In the

32

Verse 2:
In the city's melted furnace, unexpectedly we watched
With faces hidden while the walls were tightening
As the echo of the wedding bells before the blowin' rain
Dissolved into the bells of the lightning
Tolling for the rebel, tolling for the rake
Tolling for the luckless, the abandoned an' forsaked
Tolling for the outcast, burnin' constantly at stake
An' we gazed upon the chimes of freedom flashing

Verse 3:
Through the mad mystic hammering of the wild ripping hail
The sky cracked its poems in naked wonder
That the clinging of the church bells blew far into the breeze
Leaving only bells of lightning and its thunder
Striking for the gentle, striking for the kind
Striking for the guardians and protectors of the mind
An' the unpawned painter behind beyond his rightful time
An' we gazed upon the chimes of freedom flashing

Verse 4:
Through the wild cathedral evening the rain unraveled tales
For the disrobed faceless forms of no position
Tolling for the tongues with no place to bring their thoughts
All down in taken-for-granted situations
Tolling for the deaf an' blind, tolling for the mute
Tolling for the mistreated, mateless mother, the mistitled prostitute
For the misdemeanor outlaw, chased an' cheated by pursuit
An' we gazed upon the chimes of freedom flashing

Verse 5:
Even though a cloud's white curtain in a far-off corner flashed
An' the hypnotic splattered mist was slowly lifting
Electric light still struck like arrows, fired but for the ones
Condemned to drift or else be kept from drifting
Tolling for the searching ones, on their speechless, seeking trail
For the lonesome-hearted lovers with too personal a tale
An' for each unharmful, gentle soul misplaced inside a jail
An' we gazed upon the chimes of freedom flashing

Verse 6:
Starry-eyed an' laughing as I recall when we were caught
Trapped by no track of hours for they hanged suspended
As we listened one last time an' we watched with one last look
Spellbound an' swallowed 'til the tolling ended
Tolling for the aching ones whose wounds cannot be nursed
For the countless confused, accused, misused, strung-out ones an' worse
An' for every hung-up person in the whole wide universe
An' we gazed upon the chimes of freedom flashing

The Times They Are A-Changin'

Words & Music by Bob Dylan

Moderately

1. Come gath-er 'round peo-ple wher-ev-er you roam And ad-
(Verses 2-5 see block lyrics)

-mit that the wa-ters a-round you have grown And ac-cept it that

soon you'll be drenched to the bone. If your time to you is worth

sav-in' Then you bet-ter start swim-min' or you'll sink like a

stone For the times they are a-chang -

1-4.

5.

- in'_____ 2, 3, 4. Come - in'_____
5. The

34

Verse 2:
Come writers and critics
Who prophesize with your pen
And keep your eyes wide
The chance won't come again
And don't speak too soon
For the wheel's still in spin
And there's no tellin' who that it's namin'
For the loser now will be later to win
For the times they are a-changin'

Verse 3:
Come senators, congressmen
Please heed the call
Don't stand in the doorway
Don't block up the hall
For he that gets hurt
Will be he who has stalled
There's a battle outside and it is ragin'
It'll soon shake your windows and rattle your walls
For the times they are a-changin'

Verse 4:
Come mothers and fathers
Throughout the land
And don't criticize
What you can't understand
Your sons and your daughters
Are beyond your command
Your old road is rapidly agin'
Please get out of the new one if you can't lend your hand
For the times they are a-changin'

Verse 5:
The line it is drawn
The curse it is cast
The slow one now
Will later be fast
As the present now
Will later be past
The order is rapidly fadin'
And the first one now will later be last
For the times they are a-changin'

One Too Many Mornings

Words & Music by Bob Dylan

Brightly

1. Down the street the dogs are bark - in' And the day is a-get-tin'
(Verses 2 & 3 see block lyrics)

dark. As the night comes in a - fall - in', The dogs -'ll lose their

bark, An' the si - lent night will shat - ter From the

sounds in - side my mind, For I'm one too ma - ny

Play 3 times

morn - ings___ And a thou-sand miles___ be - hind. 2. From the

Verse 2:
From the crossroads of my doorstep
My eyes they start to fade
As I turn my head back to the room
Where my love and I have laid
An' I gaze back to the street
The sidewalk and the sign
And I'm one too many mornings
An' a thousand miles behind

Verse 3:
It's a restless hungry feeling
That don't mean no one no good
When ev'rythIng I'm a-sayin'
You can say it just as good
You're right from your side
I'm right from mine
We're both just one too many mornings
An' a thousand miles behind

All I Really Want To Do

Words & Music by Bob Dylan

Moderately brightly

Capo fret 2

Verse

1. I ain't look-in' to com-pete with you, Beat or
(Verses 2-6 see block lyrics)

cheat or mis-treat you, Sim-pli-fy you, clas-si-

-fy you, De-ny, de-fy or cru-ci-fy you.

Chorus

All I real-ly want to

(falsetto)

do Is, ba-by, be

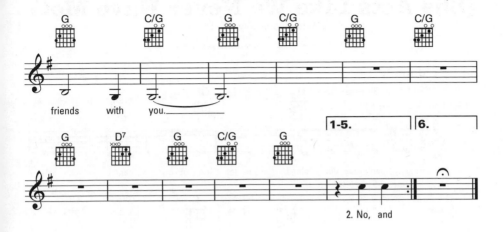

friends   with   you.____

1-5.   **6.**

2. No, and

Verse 2:
No, and I ain't lookin' to fight with you
Frighten you or tighten you
Drag you down or drain you down
Chain you down or bring you down
Chorus:

Verse 3:
I ain't lookin' to block you up
Shock or knock or lock you up
Analyze you, categorize you
Finalize you or advertise you
Chorus:

Verse 4:
I don't want to straight-face you
Race or chase you, track or trace you
Or disgrace you or displace you
Or define you or confine you
Chorus:

Verse 5:
I don't want to meet your kin
Make you spin or do you in
Or select you or dissect you
Or inspect you or reject you
Chorus:

Verse 6:
I don't want to fake you out
Take or shake or forsake you out
I ain't lookin' for you to feel like me
See like me or be like me
Chorus:

39

I Don't Believe You
(She Acts Like We Never Have Met)

Words & Music by Bob Dylan

Brightly

1. I can't un-der-stand, She let go of my hand An'
(Verses 2-5 see block lyrics)

left me here fac-ing the wall. I'd sure like t' know

Why she did go, But I can't get close t' her at all.

Though we kissed through the wild blaz-ing night-time, She said

she would nev-er for-get. But now morn-in's clear, It's

like I ain't here, She just acts like we nev-er have met. *Play 5 times*

2. It's

40

Verse 2:
It's all new t' me
Like some mystery
It could even be like a myth
Yet it's hard t' think on
That she's the same one
That last night I was with
From darkness, dreams're deserted
Am I still dreamin' yet?
I wish she'd unlock
Her voice once an' talk
'Stead of acting like we never have met

Verse 3:
If she ain't feelin' well
Then why don't she tell
'Stead of turnin' her back t' my face?
Without any doubt
She seems too far out
For me t' return t' her chase
Though the night ran swirling an' whirling
I remember her whispering yet
But evidently she don't
An' evidently she won't
She just acts like we never have met

Verse 4:
If I didn't have t' guess
I'd gladly confess
T' anything I might've tried
If I was with 'er too long
Or have done something wrong
I wish she'd tell me what it is, I'll run an' hide
Though her skirt it swayed as a guitar played
Her mouth was watery and wet
But now something has changed
For she ain't the same
She just acts like we never have met

Verse 5:
I'm leavin' today
I'll be on my way
Of this I can't say very much
But if you want me to
I can be just like you
An' pretend that we never have touched
An' if anybody asks me
"Is it easy to forget?"
I'll say, "It's easily done
You just pick anyone
An' pretend that you never have met!"

Spanish Harlem Incident

Words & Music by Bob Dylan

1. Gyp - sy   gal,_____ the hands of Har - lem   Can - not hold
(Verses 2 & 3 see block lyrics)

_____ you to its heat.___ Your tem - pera - ture's too hot for tam - ing___ Your flam - ing

feet burn up the street____   I am home - less come and take_ me

In - to reach of your rat - tling drums.   Let me know, babe,   a - bout my

for - tune Down a - long my rest - less palms.____

Play 3 times

2. Gyp - sy

42

Verse 2:
Gypsy gal, you got me swallowed
I have fallen far beneath
Your pearly eyes, so fast an' slashing
An' your flashing diamond teeth
The night is pitch black, come an' make my
Pale face fit into place, ah, please!
Let me know, babe, I'm nearly drowning
If it's you my lifelines trace

Verse 3:
I been wond'rin' all about me
Ever since I seen you there
On the cliffs of your wildcat charms I'm riding
I know I'm 'round you but I don't know where
You have slayed me, you have made me
I got to laugh halfways off my heels
I got to know, babe, will you surround me?
So I can tell if I'm really real

My Back Pages

Words & Music by Bob Dylan

Moderately (freely)

Capo fret 3

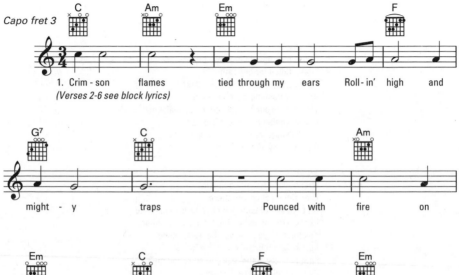

1. Crim - son flames tied through my ears Roll- in' high and
(Verses 2-6 see block lyrics)

might - y traps Pounced with fire on

flam - ing roads Us - ing i - deas as my

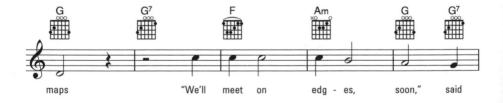

maps "We'll meet on edg - es, soon," said

I, Proud 'neath heat - ed brow._____ Ah, but

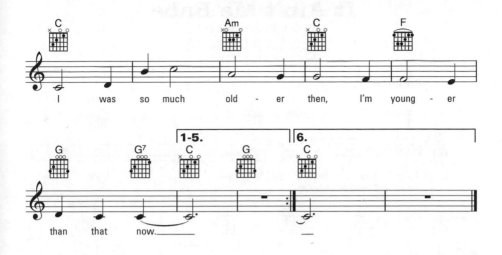

I was so much old - er then, I'm young - er

than that now._____

1-5.

6.

Verse 2:
Half-wracked prejudice leaped forth
"Rip down all hate," I screamed
Lies that life is black and white
Spoke from my skull. I dreamed
Romantic facts of musketeers
Foundationed deep, somehow
Ah, but I was so much older then
I'm younger than that now

Verse 3:
Girls' faces formed the forward path
From phony jealousy
To memorizing politics
Of ancient history
Flung down by corpse evangelists
Unthought of, though, somehow
Ah, but I was so much older then
I'm younger than that now

Verse 4:
A self-ordained professor's tongue
Too serious to fool
Spouted out that liberty
Is just equality in school
"Equality," I spoke the word
As if a wedding vow
Ah, but I was so much older then
I'm younger than that now

Verse 5:
In a soldier's stance, I aimed my hand
At the mongrel dogs who teach
Fearing not that I'd become my enemy
In the instant that I preach
My pathway led by confusion boats
Mutiny from stern to bow
Ah, but I was so much older then
I'm younger than that now

Verse 6:
Yes, my guard stood hard when abstract threats
Too noble to neglect
Deceived me into thinking
I had something to protect
Good and bad, I define these terms
Quite clear, no doubt, somehow
Ah, but I was so much older then
I'm younger than that now

It Ain't Me Babe

Words & Music by Bob Dylan

1. Go 'way from my win-dow,_____ Leave at your
(Verses 2 & 3 see block lyrics)
own cho-sen speed. I'm not the
one you want, babe,_____ I'm not the one you____
need. You say you're look - in' for some -
- one____ Nev - er___ weak but al - ways strong,_____ To pro -
- tect you an' de - fend you_____ Whe - ther you are right or

wrong,_____ Some - one to op-en each and ev-'ry door,_____

Chorus

_____ But it ain't me, babe,_____ No, no, no,_____ it ain't me, babe,_

_____ It ain't me you're look-in' for,_ babe._____

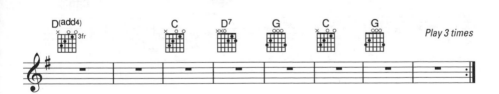

Play 3 times

Verse 2:
Go lightly from the ledge, babe
Go lightly on the ground
I'm not the one you want, babe
I will only let you down
You say you're lookin' for someone
Who will promise never to part
Someone to close his eyes for you
Someone to close his heart
Someone who will die for you an' more
But it ain't me, babe
No, no, no, it ain't me, babe
It ain't me you're lookin' for, babe

Verse 3:
Go melt back into the night, babe
Everything inside is made of stone
There's nothing in here moving
An' anyway I'm not alone
You say you're looking for someone
Who'll pick you up each time you fall
To gather flowers constantly
An' to come each time you call
A lover for your life an' nothing more
But it ain't me, babe
No, no, no, it ain't me, babe
It ain't me you're lookin' for, babe

47

To Ramona

Words & Music by Bob Dylan

Moderately

1. Ra - mo - na__ come clo - ser,_ Shut soft-ly__ your wa - ter - y eyes.____
(Verses 2-5 see block lyrics)

The pangs of your_ sad-ness Shall pass as your

sen - ses will rise.____ The flow - ers__ of the

ci - ty,__ Though breath - like, get death-like at times.____

And there's_ no use in try - in' T' deal with the

Play 5 times

dy - in',__ Though I can - not__ ex - plain that in lines.____ 2. Your

Verse 2:
Your cracked country lips
I still wish to kiss
As to be under the strength of your skin
Your magnetic movements
Still capture the minutes I'm in
But it grieves my heart, love
To see you tryin' to be a part of
A world that just don't exist
It's all just a dream, babe
A vacuum, a scheme, babe
That sucks you into feelin' like this

Verse 3:
I can see that your head
Has been twisted and fed
By worthless foam from the mouth
I can tell you are torn
Between stayin' and returnin'
On back to the South
You've been fooled into thinking
That the finishin' end is at hand
Yet there's no one to beat you
No one t' defeat you
'Cept the thoughts of yourself feeling bad

Verse 4:
I've heard you say many times
That you're better 'n no one
And no one is better 'n you
If you really believe that
You know you got
Nothing to win and nothing to lose
From fixtures and forces and friends
Your sorrow does stem
That hype you and type you
Making you feel
That you must be exactly like them

Verse 5:
I'd forever talk to you
But soon my words
They would turn into a meaningless ring
For deep in my heart
I know there is no help I can bring
Everything passes
Everything changes
Just do what you think you should do
And someday maybe
Who knows, baby
I'll come and be cryin' to you

Plugged In

The mythology of Dylan's 'sell-out' to the forces of rock, fame and fortune is well known. The relevant material, though, obviously reflected a burst of fresh creativity. The transitional album was *Bringing It All Back Home (1965)*; it was half electric and half acoustic... but all original. 'It's All Over Now Baby Blue', 'Subterranean Homesick Blues' and 'Mr. Tambourine Man' all spilled out to thrill or disappoint, depending on how you happened to feel about last year's Dylan model. *Highway 61 Revisited (1965)* was all-electric, rough-sounding and memorable. It introduced 'Like A Rolling Stone' and the first of Dylan's long story songs 'Desolation Row', a freakish 11-minute tour of his vision of a hell-on-earth thoroughfare populated with writers and artists and circus performers. The abrasive hit 'Positively 4th Street' was recorded at the same time.

Subterranean Homesick Blues

Words & Music by Bob Dylan

Verse 2:
Maggie comes fleet foot
Face full of black soot
Talkin' that the heat put
Plants in the bed but
The phone's tapped anyway
Maggie says that many say
They must bust in early May
Orders from the D. A.
Look out kid
Don't matter what you did
Walk on your tip toes
Don't try "No Doz"
Better stay away from those
That carry around a fire hose
Keep a clean nose
Watch the plain clothes
You don't need a weather man
To know which way the wind blows

Verse 3:
Get sick, get well
Hang around a ink well
Ring bell, hard to tell
If anything is goin' to sell
Try hard, get barred
Get back, write braille
Get jailed, jump bail
Join the army, if you fail
Look out kid
You're gonna get hit
But users, cheaters
Six-time losers
Hang around the theaters
Girl by the whirlpool
Lookin' for a new fool
Don't follow leaders
Watch the parkin' meters

Verse 4:
 Ah get born, keep warm
Short pants, romance, learn to dance
Get dressed, get blessed
Try to be a success
Please her, please him, buy gifts
Don't steal, don't lift
Twenty years of schoolin'
And they put you on the day shift
Look out kid
They keep it all hid
Better jump down a manhole
Light yourself a candle
Don't wear sandals
Try to avoid the scandals
Don't wanna be a bum
You better chew gum
The pump don't work
 'Cause the vandals took the handles

Maggie's Farm

Words & Music by Bob Dylan

Brightly

Capo fret 3

1. I ain't gon - na work on Mag-gie's farm no more.___
(Verses 2-5 see block lyrics)

No, I ain't gon - na work on Mag-gie's farm no more.___

Well, I wake in the morn - ing, Fold my hands and pray for

rain. I got a head full of i - de - as___ That are driv - in' me in -

- sane. It's a shame the way she makes me scrub the floor. I

ain't gon - na work on Mag-gie's farm no more.___ 2. I

Play 5 times

54

Verse 2:
I ain't gonna work for Maggie's brother no more
No, I ain't gonna work for Maggie's brother no more
Well, he hands you a nickel
He hands you a dime
He asks you with a grin
If you're havin' a good time
Then he fines you every time you slam the door
I ain't gonna work for Maggie's brother no more

Verse 3:
I ain't gonna work for Maggie's pa no more
No, I ain't gonna work for Maggie's pa no more
Well, he puts his cigar
Out in your face just for kicks
His bedroom window
It is made out of bricks
The National Guard stands around his door
Ah, I ain't gonna work for Maggie's pa no more

Verse 4:
I ain't gonna work for Maggie's ma no more
No, I ain't gonna work for Maggie's ma no more
Well, she talks to all the servants
About man and God and law
Everybody says
She's the brains behind pa
She's sixty-eight, but she says she's twenty-four
I ain't gonna work for Maggie's ma no more

Verse 5:
I ain't gonna work on Maggie's farm no more
No, I ain't gonna work on Maggie's farm no more
Well, I try my best
To be just like I am
But everybody wants you
To be just like them
They sing while you slave and I just get bored
I ain't gonna work on Maggie's farm no more

Mr. Tambourine Man

Words & Music by Bob Dylan

Moderately

Capo fret 3

Chorus

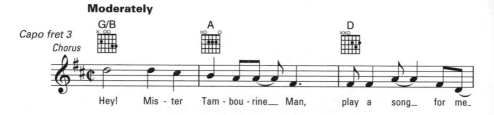

Hey! Mis - ter Tam - bou - rine_ Man, play a song_ for me_

_ I'm not sleep - y and there is_____ no___ place_ I'm

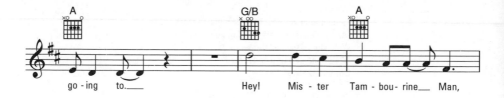

go - ing to.___ Hey! Mis - ter Tam - bou - rine_ Man,

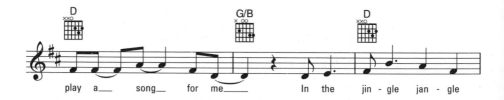

play a__ song__ for me___ In the jin - gle jan - gle

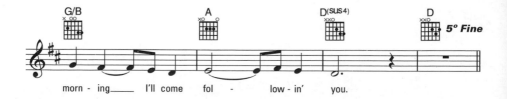

morn - ing_____ I'll come fol - low - in' you.

Verse

G/B A D

1. Though I know that eve - nin's em - pire has re - turned in - to
(Verses 2-4 see block lyrics)

G/B D G/B D

sand, Van -ished from my hand, Left me blind - ly here_ to_ stand_

G/B Em A A(SUS4) A G/B

___ but_ still_ not sleep - ing. My wear - i - ness a - maz -

A D G/B

- es me,_ I'm brand - ed on_ my_ feet,____ I

D G/B D

have no_ one_ to meet_ And the an - cient_ emp - ty_ street's_

Play 4 times

G/B Em A A(SUS4) A

___ too_ dead_ for dream - ing.

57

Verse 2:
Take me on a trip upon your magic swirlin' ship
My senses have been stripped, my hands can't feel to grip
My toes too numb to step
Wait only for my boot heels to be wanderin'
I'm ready to go anywhere, I'm ready for to fade
Into my own parade, cast your dancing spell my way
I promise to go under it
Chorus:

Verse 3:
Though you might hear laughin', spinnin', swingin' madly across the sun
It's not aimed at anyone, it's just escapin' on the run
And but for the sky there are no fences facin'
And if you hear vague traces of skippin' reels of rhyme
To your tambourine in time, it's just a ragged clown behind
I wouldn't pay it any mind
It's just a shadow you're seein' that he's chasing
Chorus:

Verse 4:
Then take me disappearin' through the smoke rings of my mind
Down the foggy ruins of time, far past the frozen leaves
The haunted, frightened trees, out to the windy beach
Far from the twisted reach of crazy sorrow
Yes, to dance beneath the diamond sky with one hand waving free
Silhouetted by the sea, circled by the circus sands
With all memory and fate driven deep beneath the waves
Let me forget about today until tomorrow
Chorus:

It's Alright, Ma (I'm Only Bleeding)

Words & Music by Bob Dylan

Medium bright

1. Dark-ness at the break of noon Shad-ows ev-en the sil-ver spoon The
(Verses 2-5 see block lyrics)

hand-made blade, the child's bal-loon E-clip-ses both the sun and moon To

un-der-stand you know too soon, There is no sense in try-ing.

Point-ed threats, they bluff with scorn Su-i-cide re-marks are torn From the fool's gold

mouth-piece the hol-low horn Plays wast-ed words, proves to warn That

he not bu-sy be-ing born_____ Is bu-sy dy-ing.

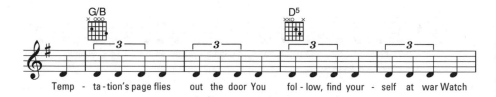

Temp - ta-tion's page flies out the door You fol-low, find your-self at war Watch

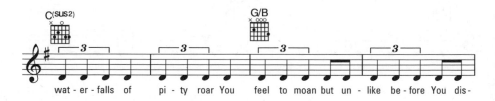

wat-er-falls of pi-ty roar You feel to moan but un-like be-fore You dis-

- cov-er that you'd just be one more Per-son cry-ing.

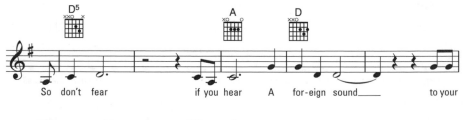

So don't fear if you hear A for-eign sound_____ to your

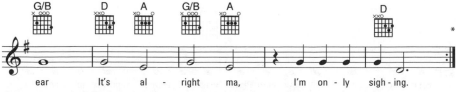

ear It's al-right ma, I'm on-ly sigh-ing.

The asterisks denote ad lib guitar breaks which occur at these points in the Dylan recording.

As some warn victory, some downfall
Private reasons great or small
Can be seen in the eyes of those that call
To make all that should be killed to crawl
While others say don't hate nothing at all
Except hatred

Disillusioned words like bullets bark
As human gods aim for their mark
Made everything from toy guns that spark
To flesh-colored Christs that glow in the dark
It's easy to see without looking too far
That not much is really sacred

While preachers preach of evil fates
Teachers teach that knowledge waits
Can lead to hundred-dollar plates
Goodness hides behind its gates
But even the president of the United States
Sometimes must have to stand naked

An' though the rules of the road have been lodged
It's only people's games that you got to dodge
And it's alright, Ma, I can make it

Verse 3:
Advertising signs that con
You into thinking you're the one
That can do what's never been done
That can win what's never been won
Meantime life outside goes on
All around you

You lose yourself, you reappear
You suddenly find you got nothing to fear
Alone you stand with nobody near
When a trembling distant voice, unclear
Startles your sleeping ears to hear
That somebody thinks they really found you

A question in your nerves is lit
Yet you know there is no answer fit
To satisfy insure you not to quit
To keep it in your mind and not forget
That it is not he or she or them or it
That you belong to

Although the masters make the rules
For the wise men and the fools
I got nothing, Ma, to live up to

Verse 4:
For them that must obey authority
That they do not respect in any degree
Who despise their jobs, their destinies
Speak jealously of them that are free
Cultivate their flowers to be
Nothing more than something they invest in

While some on principles baptized
To strict party platform ties
Social clubs in drag disguise
Outsiders they can freely criticize
Tell nothing except who to idolize
And then say God bless him

While one who sings with his tongue on fire
Gargles in the rat race choir
Bent out of shape from society's pliers
Cares not to come up any higher
But rather get you down in the hole
That he's in

But I mean no harm nor put fault
On anyone that lives in a vault
But it's alright, Ma, if I can't please him

Verse 5:
Old lady judges watch people in pairs
Limited in sex, they dare
To push fake morals, insult and stare
While money doesn't talk, it swears
Obscenity, who really cares
Propaganda, all is phony

While them that defend what they cannot see
With a killer's pride, security
It blows the minds most bitterly
For them that think death's honesty
Won't fall upon them naturally
Life sometimes must get lonely

My eyes collide head-on with stuffed
Graveyards false gods, I scuff
At pettiness which plays so rough
Walk upside-down inside handcuffs
Kick my legs to crash it off
Say okay, I have had enough what else can you show me?

And if my thought-dreams could be seen
They'd probably put my head in a guillotine
But it's alright, Ma, it's life, and life only

61

Gates Of Eden

Words & Music by Bob Dylan

Moderately

1. Of war and peace the truth just twists Its cur-few gull just

(Verses 2-9 see block lyrics)

glides Up - on four - leg - ged

for - est clouds The cow - boy an - gel rides

With his can - dle lit in - to the sun Though its

glow is waxed in black All ex -

Play 9 times

-cept when 'neath the trees of E - den

2. The

Verse 2:
The lamppost stands with folded arms
Its iron claws attached
To curbs 'neath holes where babies wail
Though it shadows metal badge
All and all can only fall
With a crashing but meaningless blow
No sound ever comes from the Gates of Eden

Verse 3:
The savage soldier sticks his head in sand
And then complains
Unto the shoeless hunter who's gone deaf
But still remains
Upon the beach where hound dogs bay
At ships with tattooed sails
Heading for the Gates of Eden

Verse 4:
With a time-rusted compass blade
Aladdin and his lamp
Sits with Utopian hermit monks
Side saddle on the Golden Calf
And on their promises of paradise
You will not hear a laugh
All except inside the Gates of Eden

Verse 5:
Relationships of ownership
They whisper in the wings
To those condemned to act accordingly
And wait for succeeding kings
And I try to harmonize with songs
The lonesome sparrow sings
There are no kings inside the Gates of Eden

Verse 6:
The motorcycle black madonna
Two-wheeled gypsy queen
And her silver-studded phantom cause
The gray flannel dwarf to scream
As he weeps to wicked birds of prey
Who pick up on his bread crumb sins
And there are no sins inside the Gates of Eden

Verse 7:
The kingdoms of Experience
In the precious wind they rot
While paupers change possessions
Each one wishing for what the other has got
And the princess and the prince
Discuss what's real and what is not
It doesn't matter inside the Gates of Eden

Verse 8:
The foreign sun, it squints upon
A bed that is never mine
As friends and other strangers
From their fates try to resign
Leaving men wholly, totally free
To do anything they wish to do but die
And there are no trials inside the Gates of Eden

Verse 9:
At dawn my lover comes to me
And tells me of her dreams
With no attempts to shovel the glimpse
Into the ditch of what each one means
At times I think there are no words
But these to tell what's true
And there are no truths outside the Gates of Eden

Love Minus Zero/No Limit

Words & Music by Bob Dylan

Moderately

Capo fret 4

1. My love,_____ she speaks like si - lence,
(Verses 2-4 see block lyrics)
with-out i - deals or vio - lence. She does-n't have to say she's faith - ful, yet she's true,_____ like ice,_____ like fire.

Peo - ple car - ry ros - es, Make prom-is-es by the hours, My love she laughs like the flow - ers, Val - en -

-tines can't buy her. *Play 4 times* 2. In the *Repeat to fade*

Verse 2:

In the dime stores and bus stations
People talk of situations
Read books, repeat quotations
Draw conclusions on the wall
Some speak of the future
My love, she speaks softly
She knows there's no success like failure
And that failure's no success at all

Verse 3:

The cloak and dagger dangles
Madams light the candles
In ceremonies of the horsemen
Even the pawn must hold a grudge
Statues made of matchsticks
Crumble into one another
My love winks, she does not bother
She knows too much to argue or to judge

Verse 4:

The bridge at midnight trembles
The country doctor rambles
Bankers' nieces seek perfection
Expecting all the gifts that wise men bring
The wind howls like a hammer
The night blows cold and rainy
My love she's like some raven
At my window with a broken wing

She Belongs To Me

Words & Music by Bob Dylan

Moderately

Capo fret 2

1. She's got ev-'ry-thing__ she needs, She's an ar-tist she don't look
(Verses 2-5 see block lyrics)

back. She's got ev-'ry-thing__ she needs, She's an

ar-tist she don't look back.

She can take the dark out of the night-time And__

__ paint the day-time black.

Play 5 times

2. You will

66

It's All Over Now, Baby Blue

Verse 2:
You will start out standing
Proud to steal her anything she sees
You will start out standing
Proud to steal her anything she sees
But you will wind up peeking through her keyhole
Down upon your knees

Verse 3:
She never stumbles
She's got no place to fall
She never stumbles
She's got no place to fall
She's nobody's child
The Law can't touch her at all

Verse 4:
She wears an Egyptian ring
That sparkles before she speaks
She wears an Egyptian ring
That sparkles before she speaks
She's a hypnotist collector
You are a walking antique

Verse 5:
Bow down to her on Sunday
Salute her when her birthday comes
Bow down to her on Sunday
Salute her when her birthday comes
For Halloween give her a trumpet
And for Christmas, buy her a drum

It's All Over Now, Baby Blue

Words & Music by Bob Dylan

Medium slow

Capo fret 4

1. You must leave__ now, take what you need, you think will last.__ But what-

(Verses 2-4 see block lyrics)

-ev-er you wish to keep, you bet-ter grab it fast.__

Yon-der stands your or-phan, with his gun,__

Cry-ing like a fire__ in the sun.__ Look out the__

saints are com-in' through__ And it's all ov-er

1-4.   **5.**

now, Ba-by Blue.__

68

Verse 2:
The highway is for gamblers, better use your sense
Take what you have gathered from coincidence
The empty-handed painter from your streets
Is drawing crazy patterns on your sheets
This sky, too, is folding under you
And it's all over now, Baby Blue

Verse 3:
All your seasick sailors, they are rowing home
All your reindeer armies, are all going home
The lover who just walked out your door
Has taken all his blankets from the floor
The carpet, too, is moving under you
And it's all over now, Baby Blue

Verse 4:
Instrumental

Verse 5:
Leave your stepping stones behind, something calls for you
Forget the dead you've left, they will not follow you
The vagabond who's rapping at your door
Is standing in the clothes that you once wore
Strike another match, go start anew
And it's all over now, Baby Blue

Like A Rolling Stone

Words & Music by Bob Dylan

Brightly

1. Once up - on___ a time you dressed so fine___ You threw the bums a dime

(Verses 2-4 see block lyrics)

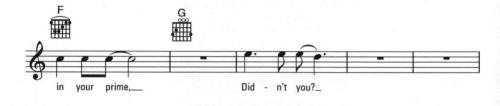

in your prime,___ Did - n't you?___

Peo - ple'd call, say, "Be - ware doll, you're bound to fall,"_ You thought they were all

kid - din' you___ You used to

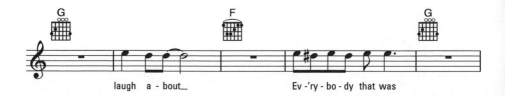

laugh a - bout___ Ev -'ry - bo - dy that was

70

hang-in' out___   Now you don't   talk so   loud

Now you   don't   seem so proud   A - bout   hav-ing to be

scroung - ing   for   your   next   meal._____

Chorus

How does it   feel   How does it   feel

{ To be with-out a   home }
{ With no di-rec-tion home }

Like a com-plete un - known   Like a roll - ing   stone?

Play 4 times   *Repeat to fade*

71

Verse 2:
You've gone to the finest school all right, Miss Lonely
But you know you only used to get juiced in it
And nobody has ever taught you how to live on the street
And now you find out you're gonna have to get used to it
You said you'd never compromise
With the mystery tramp, but now you realize
He's not selling any alibis
As you stare into the vacuum of his eyes
And ask him do you want to make a deal?
Chorus:

Verse 3:
You never turned around to see the frowns on the jugglers and the clowns
When they all come down and did tricks for you
You never understood that it ain't no good
You shouldn't let other people get your kicks for you
You used to ride on the chrome horse with your diplomat
Who carried on his shoulder a Siamese cat
Ain't it hard when you discover that
He really wasn't where it's at
After he took from you everything he could steal
Chorus:

Verse 4:
Princess on the steeple and all the pretty people
They're drinkin', thinkin' that they got it made
Exchanging all kinds of precious gifts and things
But you'd better lift your diamond ring, you'd better pawn it babe
You used to be so amused
At Napoleon in rags and the language that he used
Go to him now, he calls you, you can't refuse
When you got nothing, you got nothing to lose
You're invisible now, you got no secrets to conceal
Chorus:

Tombstone Blues

Words & Music by Bob Dylan

Brightly

Capo fret 2

1. The sweet pret-ty things are in bed now of course The
(Verses 2-6 see block lyrics)

ci - ty fa - thers they're try - ing to en - dorse_____ The

re - in - car - na - tion of Paul Re - vere's horse But the

town has no need to be ner - vous

The ghost of Belle Starr she hands down her wits To

Je - ze - bel the nun she vi - o - lent - ly knits_____ A

73

bald wig for Jack the Rip - per_____ who sits at the

head of the cham - ber of com - merce

Chorus

Ma-ma's in the fact-'ry She ain't got no shoes___ Dad-dy's in the

al - ley He's look - in' for the fuse, I'm in the streets With the

tomb-stone blues___ 2. The

Verse 2:
The hysterical bride in the penny arcade
Screaming she moans, "I've just been made"
Then sends out for the doctor who pulls down the shade
Says, "My advice is to not let the boys in"
Now the medicine man comes and he shuffles inside
He walks with a swagger and he says to the bride
"Stop all this weeping, swallow your pride
You will not die, it's not poison"
Chorus:

Verse 3:
Well, John the Baptist after torturing a thief
Looks up at his hero the Commander-in-Chief
Saying, "Tell me great hero, but please make it brief
Is there a hole for me to get sick in?"
The Commander-in-Chief answers him while chasing a fly
Saying, "Death to all those who would whimper and cry"
And dropping a barbell he points to the sky
Saying, "The sun's not yellow it's chicken"
Chorus:

Verse 4:
The king of the Philistines his soldiers to save
Puts jawbones on their tombstones and flatters their graves
Puts the pied pipers in prison and fattens the slaves
Then sends them out to the jungle
Gypsy Davey with a blowtorch he burns out their camps
With his faithful slave Pedro behind him he tramps
With a fantastic collection of stamps
To win friends and influence his uncle
Chorus:

Verse 5:
The geometry of innocence flesh on the bone
Causes Galileo's math book to get thrown
At Delilah who sits worthlessly alone
But the tears on her cheeks are from laughter
Now I wish I could give Brother Bill his great thrill
I would set him in chains at the top of the hill
Then send out for some pillars and Cecil B. DeMille
He could die happily ever after
Chorus:

Verse 6:
Where Ma Rainey and Beethoven once unwrapped their bedroll
Tuba players now rehearse around the flagpole
And the National Bank at a profit sells road maps for the soul
To the old folks home and the college
Now I wish I could write you a melody so plain
That could hold you dear lady from going insane
That could ease you and cool you and cease the pain
Of your useless and pointless knowledge
Chorus:

It Takes A Lot To Laugh, It Takes A Train To Cry

Words & Music by Bob Dylan

Medium slow blues

Capo fret 1

1. Well, I ride on a mail-train, ba-by, Can't buy a thrill.
(Verses 2 & 3 see block lyrics)

Well, I've been up all night, ba-by

Lean-in' on the win-dow-sill. Well, if I die on

top of the hill And if I don't make it

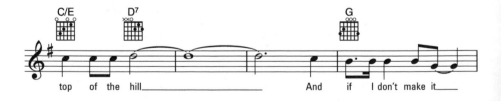

Play 3 times

You know my ba-by will. 2. Don't the

76

Verse 2:
Don't the moon look good, mama
Shinin' through the trees?
Don't the brakeman look good, mama
Flagging down the "Double E?"
Don't the sun look good
Goin' down over the sea?
Don't my gal look fine
When she's comin' after me?

Verse 3:
Now the wintertime is coming
The windows are filled with frost
I went to tell everybody
But I could not get across
Well, I wanna be your lover, baby
I don't wanna be your boss
Don't say I never warned you
When your train gets lost

Highway 61 Revisited

Words & Music by Bob Dylan

Brightly

Capo fret 1

1. Oh God said to A-bra-ham, "Kill me a son," Abe says, "Man you must be

(Verses 2-5 see block lyrics)

put-tin' me on."__ God say, "No." Abe say, "What?"

God say, "You can do what you want Abe, but the next time you see me

com-in' you bet-ter run." Well

Abe says, "Where do you want this kill-in' done?" God says, "Out on High-way

Play 5 times

Six-ty - one." 2. Well

78

Verse 2:
Well Georgia Sam he had a bloody nose
Welfare Department they wouldn't give him no clothes
He asked poor Howard where can I go
Howard said there's only one place I know
Sam said tell me quick man I got to run
Ol' Howard just pointed with his gun
And said that way down on Highway 61

Verse 3:
Well Mack the Finger said to Louie the King
I got forty red, white and blue shoestrings
And a thousand telephones that don't ring
Do you know where I can get rid of these things
And Louie the King said let me think for a minute son
And he said yes I think it can be easily done
Just take everything down to Highway 61

Verse 4:
Now the fifth daughter on the twelfth night
Told the first father that things weren't right
My complexion she said is much too white
He said come here and step into the light, he says hmm you're right
Let me tell the second mother this has been done
But the second mother was with the seventh son
And they were both out on Highway 61

Verse 5:
Now the rovin' gambler he was very bored
He was tryin' to create a next world war
He found a promoter who nearly fell off the floor
He said I never engaged in this kind of thing before
But yes I think it can be very easily done
We'll just put some bleachers out in the sun
And have it on Highway 61

Queen Jane Approximately

Words & Music by Bob Dylan

1. When your mo-ther___ sends back all your in-vi-ta-tions
(Verses 2-5 see block lyrics)

And your fa-ther___ to your sis-ter he ex-plains___

That you're ti-red___ of your-self and all of your cre-a-tions

Won't you come see me, Queen Jane?

Won't you come see me, Queen Jane? 2. Now when

Play 5 times

80

Verse 2:
Now when all of the flower ladies want back what they have lent you
And the smell of their roses does not remain
And all of your children start to resent you
Won't you come see me, Queen Jane?
Won't you come see me, Queen Jane?

Verse 3:
Now when all the clowns that you have commissioned
Have died In battle or in vain
And you're sick of all this repetition
Won't you come see me, Queen Jane?
Won't you come see me, Queen Jane?

Verse 4:
When all of your advisers heave their plastic
At your feet to convince you of your pain
Trying to prove that your conclusions should be more drastic
Won't you come see me, Queen Jane?
Won't you come see me, Queen Jane?

Verse 5:
Now when all the bandits that you turned your other cheek to
All lay down their bandanas and complain
And you want somebody you don't have to speak to
Won't you come see me, Queen Jane?
Won't you come see me, Queen Jane?

Just Like Tom Thumb's Blues

Words & Music by Bob Dylan

82

Verse 2:
Now if you see Saint Annie
Please tell her thanks a lot
I cannot move
My fingers are all in a knot
I don't have the strength
To get up and take another shot
And my best friend, my doctor
Won't even say what it is I've got

Verse 3:
Sweet Melinda
The peasants call her the goddess of gloom
She speaks good English
And she invites you up into her room
And you're so kind
And careful not to go to her too soon
And she takes your voice
And leaves you howling at the moon

Verse 4:
Up on Housing Project Hill
It's either fortune or fame
You must pick up one or the other
Though neither of them are to be what they claim
If you're lookin' to get silly
You better go back to from where you came
Because the cops don't need you
And man they expect the same

Verse 5:
Now all the authorities
They just stand around and boast
How they blackmailed the sergeant-at-arms
Into leaving his post
And picking up Angel who
Just arrived here from the coast
Who looked so fine at first
But left looking just like a ghost

Verse 6:
I started out on burgundy
But soon hit the harder stuff
Everybody said they'd stand behind me
When the game got rough
But the joke was on me
There was nobody even there to call my bluff
I'm going back to New York City
I do believe I've had enough

Desolation Row

Words & Music by Bob Dylan

Steadily

Capo fret 4

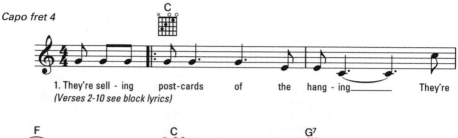

1. They're sell - ing post-cards of the hang - ing_____ They're
(Verses 2-10 see block lyrics)

paint-ing the pass - ports brown The beau - ty par- lor's filled with

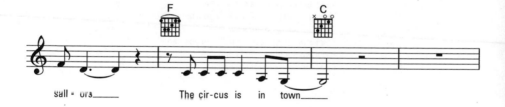

sail - ors_____ The cir-cus is in town_____

Here comes the blind com - is - sion - er_____ They've got him in a trance_____ One

hand is tied to the tight-rope walk - er_____ The oth - er is in his

pants   And the   ri - ot   squad they're rest- less   They

need   some - where to   go_____   As   La - dy   and I   look

out   to - night___ From   Des - o - la - tion   Row_____   *Play 10 times*

Verse 2:
Cinderella, she seems so easy
"It takes one to know one," she smiles
And puts her hands in her back pockets
Bette Davis style
And in comes Romeo, he's moaning
"You Belong to Me I Believe"
And someone says,"You're in the wrong place, my friend
You better leave"
And the only sound that's left
After the ambulances go
Is Cinderella sweeping up
On Desolation Row

Verse 3:
Now the moon is almost hidden
The stars are beginning to hide
The fortune-telling lady
Has even taken all her things inside
All except for Cain and Abel
And the hunchback of Notre Dame
Everybody is making love
Or else expecting rain
And the Good Samaritan, he's dressing
He's getting ready for the show
He's going to the carnival tonight
On Desolation Row

Verse 4:
Now Ophelia, she's 'neath the window
For her I feel so afraid
On her twenty-second birthday
She already is an old maid
To her, death is quite romantic
She wears an iron vest
Her profession's her religion
Her sin is her lifelessness
And though her eyes are fixed upon
Noah's great rainbow
She spends her time peeking
Into Desolation Row

Verse 5:
Einstein, disguised as Robin Hood
With his memories in a trunk
Passed this way an hour ago
With his friend, a jealous monk
He looked so immaculately frightful
As he bummed a cigarette
Then he went off sniffing drainpipes
And reciting the alphabet
Now you would not think to look at him
But he was famous long ago
For playing the electric violin
On Desolation Row

Verse 6:
Dr. Filth, he keeps his world
Inside of a leather cup
But all his sexless patients
They're trying to blow it up
Now his nurse, some local loser
She's in charge of the cyanide hole
And she also keeps the cards that read
"Have Mercy on His Soul"
They all play on pennywhistles
You can hear them blow
If you lean your head out far enough
From Desolation Row

Verse 7:
Across the street they've nailed the curtains
They're getting ready for the feast
The Phantom of the Opera
A perfect image of a priest
They're spoonfeeding Casanova
To get him to feel more assured
Then they'll kill him with self-confidence
After poisoning him with words
And the Phantom's shouting to skinny girls
"Get Outa Here If You Don't Know
Casanova is just being punished for going
To Desolation Row"

Verse 8:
Now at midnight all the agents
And the superhuman crew
Come out and round up everyone
That knows more than they do
Then they bring them to the factory
Where the heart-attack machine
Is strapped across their shoulders
And then the kerosene
Is brought down from the castles
By insurance men who go
Check to see that nobody is escaping
To Desolation Row

Verse 9:
Praise be to Nero's Neptune
The Titanic sails at dawn
And everybody's shouting
"Which Side Are You On?"
And Ezra Pound and T. S. Eliot
Fighting in the captain's tower
While calypso singers laugh at them
And fishermen hold flowers
Between the windows of the sea
Where lovely mermaids flow
And nobody has to think too much
About Desolation Row

Verse 10:
Yes, I received your letter yesterday
(About the time the doorknob broke)
When you asked how I was doing
Was that some kind of joke?
All these people that you mention
Yes, I know them they're quite lame
I had to rearrange their faces
And give them all another name
Right now I can't read too good
Don't send me no more letters, no
Not unless you mail them
From Desolation Row

Positively 4th Street

Words & Music by Bob Dylan

To match original recording, tune down one semitone

Moderately

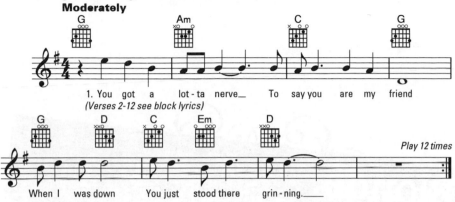

1. You got a lot-ta nerve__ To say you are my friend
(Verses 2-12 see block lyrics)

Play 12 times

When I was down You just stood there grin-ning.__

Verse 2:
You got a lotta nerve
To say you got a helping hand to lend
You just want to be on
The side that's winning

Verse 3:
You say I let you down
You know it's not like that
If you're so hurt
Why then don't you show it

Verse 4:
You say you lost your faith
But that's not where it's at
You had no faith to lose
And you know it

Verse 5:
I know the reason
That you talk behind my back
I used to be among the crowd
You're in with

Verse 6:
Do you take me for such a fool
To think I'd make contact
With the one who tries to hide
What he don't know to begin with

Verse 7:
You see me on the street
You always act surprised
You say, "How are you?" "Good luck"
But you don't mean it

Verse 8:
When you know as well as me
You'd rather see me paralyzed
Why don't you just come out once
And scream it

Verse 9:
No, I do not feel that good
When I see the heartbreaks you embrace
If I was a master thief
Perhaps I'd rob them

Verse 10:
And now I know you're dissatisfied
With your position and your place
Don't you understand
It's not my problem

Verse 11:
I wish that for just one time
You could stand inside my shoes
And just for that one moment
I could be you

Verse 12:
Yes, I wish that for just one time
You could stand inside my shoes
You'd know what a drag it is
To see you

Blonde On Blonde

This 1966 double vinyl album, that came to represent both the pinnacle and the end of Dylan's electric period was full of great songs and talented backing musicians. The opening track, 'Rainy Day Women #12 & 35' was a raucous, spaced-out blues invitation to get stoned with instrumentation suggestive of a drunken Salvation Army band. One of the album's four sides was solely occupied by 'Sad-Eyed Lady Of The Lowlands' ('the best song I ever wrote' Dylan once said) which was only a shade shorter than 'Desolation Row'. 'Visions Of Johanna' was a lovely atmospheric late-night poem set to music. 'I Want You' was perhaps Dylan's best-ever melding of surreal lyrics with a killer up-tempo pop song. *Blonde On Blonde*, with its out-of-focus portrait of Dylan on the front cover, was to become one of the most famous albums ever made. Music critic Greil Marcus wrote that it was 'the sound of a man trying to stand up in a drunken boat, and, for the moment, succeeding'. In 2003, the album was ranked No. 9 on *Rolling Stone* magazine's list of the 500 greatest albums of all time. Whatever would Dylan's follow-up act be?

Visions Of Johanna

Words & Music by Bob Dylan

Moderately

1. Ain't it just like the night to play tricks when you're try-in' to be so
(Verses 2-4 see block lyrics)

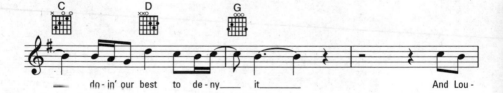

qui - et?_____ We sit here strand - ed, though we're all_

__ do-in' our best to de-ny___ it_____ And Lou-

-ise holds a hand-ful of rain, tempt-in' you_ to de - fy it_____

Lights flick-er from_ the op-po-site loft In

this room the heat pipes just cough   The coun-try mu - sic sta - tion plays soft

But there's no-thing, real-ly no-thing to turn off   Just Lou -

-ise   and her lov - er   so   en - twined

And these vi - sions_____ of Jo - han-na_____ that__

con - quer my mind__

1-3.

2. In the emp - ty

4.

5. The

ped - dler now___ speaks___ to the count - ess who's pre - tend - ing to

care for him___ Say - in', "Name me some-one that's not a par - a - site

and I'll___ go out___ and say___ a prayer_____ for him" But like Lou - ise

___ al - ways says___ "Ya can't look at much, can ya man? As she, her - self, pro -

- pares for him___ And Ma - don - na, she still___ has not

showed We see this emp - ty cage___ now cor - rode Where her

cape of the stage once had flowed   The fid-dler, he now steps to the

road   He writes ev-'ry-thing's been re-turned which was owed   On the back

of the fish truck that loads____   While my con-science ex-

-plodes   The har-mo-ni-cas play____   the

skel-e-ton keys____ and the rain____

And these vi-sions____ of Jo-han-na____

are now all that____ re-main____

Verse 2:
In the empty lot where the ladies play blindman's buff with the key chain
And the all-night girls they whisper of escapades out on the "D" train
We can hear the night watchman click his flashlight
Ask himself if it's him or them that's really insane
Louise, she's all right, she's just near
She's delicate and seems like the mirror
But she just makes it all too concise and too clear
That Johanna's not here
The ghost of 'lectricity howls in the bones of her face
Where these visions of Johanna have now taken my place

Verse 3:
Now, little boy lost, he takes himself so seriously
He brags of his misery, he likes to live dangerously
And when bringing her name up
He speaks of a farewell kiss to me
He's sure got a lotta gall to be so useless and all
Muttering small talk at the wall while I'm in the hall
How can I explain?
Oh, it's so hard to get on
And these visions of Johanna, they kept me up past the dawn

Verse 4:
Inside the museums, Infinity goes up on trial
Voices echo this is what salvation must be like after a while
But Mona Lisa musta had the highway blues
You can tell by the way she smiles
See the primitive wallflower freeze
When the jelly-faced women all sneeze
Hear the one with the mustache say, "Jeeze
I can't find my knees"
Oh, jewels and binoculars hang from the head of the mule
But these visions of Johanna, they make it all seem so cruel

One Of Us Must Know
(Sooner Or Later)

Words & Music by Bob Dylan

Moderately

Capo fret 5

1. I

did-n't mean___ to treat you so bad___

You should-n't take___ it so per-son-al___ I

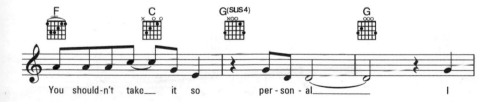

did-n't mean___ to make you so sad___

You just hap-pened to be there, that's all___

When I saw you say "good-bye"— to your friend and smile

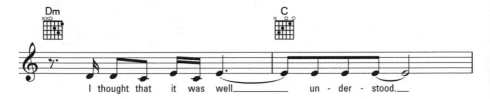

I thought that it was well_____ un-der-stood.__

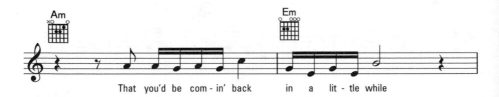

That you'd be com-in' back in a lit-tle while

I did-n't know__ that you were say-in' "good-bye"__ for good__

But,

Chorus

soon-er or lat-er, one of us__ must know You just did what you're sup-

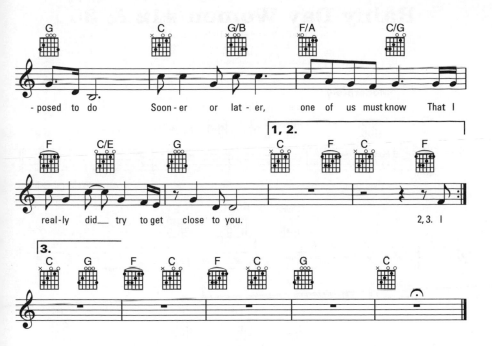

G   C   G/B   F/A   C/G

- posed to do   Soon - er   or   lat - er,   one   of   us must know   That I

F   C/E   G   **1, 2.**   C   F   C   F

real - ly did__ try to get   close to you.   2, 3. ‖

3.   C   G   F   C   F   C   G   C

Verse 2:
I couldn't see what you could show me
Your scarf had kept your mouth well hid
I couldn't see how you could know me
But you said you knew me and I believed you did
When you whispered in my ear
And asked me if I was leavin' with you or her
I didn't realize just what I did hear
I didn't realize how young you were
Chorus:

Verse 3:
I couldn't see when it started snowin'
Your voice was all that I heard
I couldn't see where we were goin'
But you said you knew an' I took your word
And then you told me later, as I apologized
That you were just kiddin' me, you weren't really from the farm
An' I told you, as you clawed out my eyes
That I never really meant to do any harm
Chorus:

Rainy Day Women #12 & 35

Words & Music by Bob Dylan

1. Well, they'll stone ya when you're tryin' to be so good, _____ They'll

(Verses 2-5 see block lyrics)

stone ya just a - like they said they would. _____ They'll

stone ya when you're tryin' to go home. _____ Then they'll

stone ya when you're there all a - lone. _____ But I

would not _____ feel _____ so all a - lone, _____

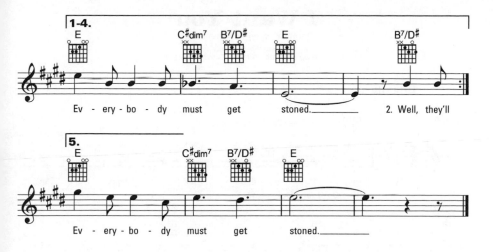

Ev - ery - bo - dy   must   get   stoned._____   2. Well, they'll

Ev - ery - bo - dy   must   get   stoned._____

Verse 2:
Well, they'll stone ya when you're walkin' 'long the street
They'll stone ya when you're tryin' to keep your seat
They'll stone ya when you're walkin' on the floor
They'll stone ya when you're walkin' to the door
But I would not feel so all alone
Everybody must get stoned

Verse 3:
They'll stone ya when you're at the breakfast table
They'll stone ya when you are young and able
They'll stone ya when you're tryin' to make a buck
They'll stone ya and then they'll say, "good luck"
Tell ya what, I would not feel so all alone
Everybody must get stoned

Verse 4:
Well, they'll stone you and say that it's the end
Then they'll stone you and then they'll come back again
They'll stone you when you're riding in your car
They'll stone you when you're playing your guitar
Yes, but I would not feel so all alone
Everybody must get stoned

Verse 5:
Well, they'll stone you when you walk all alone
They'll stone you when you are walking home
They'll stone you and then say you are brave
They'll stone you when you are set down in your grave
But I would not feel so all alone
Everybody must get stoned

I Want You

Words & Music by Bob Dylan

Brightly

Capo fret 5

1. The guilt-y un-der-tak-er sighs__ The
(Verses 2-4 see block lyrics)

lone-some or-gan grind-er cries__ The sil-ver sax-o-phones__

— say I__ should re-fuse you__ The

cracked bells and washed-out horns__ Blow in-to my

face with scorn__ But it's not that way I

was-n't born__ to lose you__ I

Chorus

C   Em/B

want you,   I want you,   I

Am   G   C

want you   so   bad   Hon-ey, I want___ you.

1, 3, 4.   **2.** *To interlude* | *Fine*

2. The   How

Interlude

Em   Am

all   my   fa-thers, they've gone   down___   True love   they've been   with-

Em   F

-out it   But   all their daugh-ters   put me down   'Cause   I don't   think   a - bout_

G   **D.S. al Fine**
                                    (Verses 3 & 4)

___   it.   3. Well,   I   re -

Verse 2:
The drunken politician leaps
Upon the street where mothers weep
And the saviours who are fast asleep, they wait for you
And I wait for them to interrupt
Me drinkin' from my broken cup
And ask me to
Open up the gate for you
I want you, I want you
I want you so bad
Honey, I want you

Verse 3:
Well, I return to the Queen of Spades
And talk with my chambermaid
She knows that I'm not afraid to look at her
She is good to me
And there's nothing she doesn't see
She knows where I'd like to be
But it doesn't matter
I want you, I want you
I want you so bad
Honey, I want you

Verse 4:
Now your dancing child with his Chinese suit
He spoke to me, I took his flute
No, I wasn't very cute to him, was I?
But I did it, though, because he lied
Because he took you for a ride
And because time was on his side
And because I...
I want you, I want you
I want you so bad
Honey, I want you

Just Like A Woman

Words & Music by Bob Dylan

Moderately slow (with a ♩ ♪ feel)

Capo fret 4

1. No - bo - dy feels an - y pain To -

(Verses 2 & 3 see block lyrics)

- night as I stand in-side the rain Ev - 'ry - bo - dy knows that

Ba - by's got new clothes But late - ly I see her

rib - bons and her bows have fall - en from her curls. She

takes just like a wo - man, yes, she does_ She makes love just like a

wo - man, yes, she does And she aches just like a

103

Verse 2:
Queen Mary she's my friend
Yes, I believe I'll go see her again
Nobody has to guess
That Baby can't be blessed
Till she sees finally that she's like all the rest
With her fog, her amphetamine and her pearls
She takes just like a woman, yes, she does
She makes love just like a woman, yes, she does
And she aches just like a woman
But she breaks just like a little girl

Verse 3:
(Ain't it clear that) I just can't fit
Yes, I believe it's time for us to quit
When we meet again
Introduced as friends
Please don't let on that you knew me when
I was hungry and it was your world
Ah, you fake just like a woman, yes, you do
You make love just like a woman, yes, you do
Then you ache just like a woman
But you break just like a little girl

Stuck Inside Of Mobile
With The Memphis Blues Again

Words & Music by Bob Dylan

106

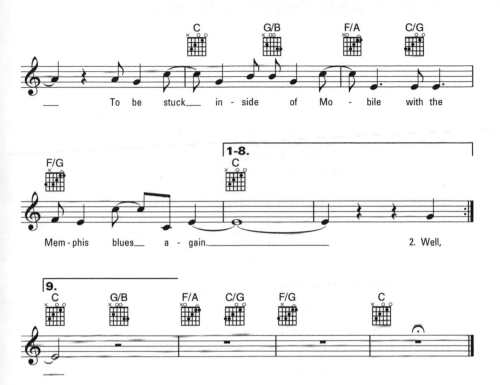

To be stuck___ in - side of Mo - bile with the

1-8.

Mem - phis blues___ a - gain._____ 2. Well,

9.

Verse 2:
Well, Shakespeare, he's in the alley
With his pointed shoes and his bells
Speaking to some French girl
Who says she knows me well
And I would send a message
To find out if she's talked
But the post office has been stolen
And the mailbox is locked
Chorus:

Verse 3:
Mona tried to tell me
To stay away from the train line
She said that all the railroad men
Just drink up your blood like wine
An' I said, "Oh, I didn't know that
But then again, there's only one I've met
An' he just smoked my eyelids
An' punched my cigarette"
Chorus:

Verse 4:
Grandpa died last week
And now he's buried in the rocks
But everybody still talks about
How badly they were shocked
But me, I expected it to happen
I knew he'd lost control
When he built a fire on Main Street
And shot it full of holes
Chorus:

Verse 5:
Now the senator came down here
Showing ev'ryone his gun
Handing out free tickets
To the wedding of his son
An' me, I nearly got busted
An' wouldn't it be my luck
To get caught without a ticket
And be discovered beneath a truck
Chorus:

Verse 6:
Now the preacher looked so baffled
When I asked him why he dressed
With twenty pounds of headlines
Stapled to his chest
But he cursed me when I proved it to him
Then I whispered, "Not even you can hide
You see, you're just like me
I hope you're satisfied"
Chorus:

Verse 7:
Now the rainman gave me two cures
Then he said, "Jump right in"
The one was Texas medicine
The other was just railroad gin
An' like a fool I mixed them
An' it strangled up my mind
An' now people just get uglier
An' I have no sense of time
Chorus:

Verse 8:
When Ruthie says come see her
In her honky-tonk lagoon
Where I can watch her waltz for free
'Neath her Panamanian moon
An' I say, "Aw come on now
You must know about my debutante"
An' she says, "Your debutante just knows what you need
But I know what you want"
Chorus:

Verse 9:
Now the bricks lay on Grand Street
Where the neon madmen climb
They all fall there so perfectly
It all seems so well timed
An' here I sit so patiently
Waiting to find out what price
You have to pay to get out of
Going through all these things twice
Chorus:

Most Likely You Go Your Way (And I'll Go Mine)

Words & Music by Bob Dylan

Moderately

1. You say you love_ me And_ you're think - in' of___ me, But you

(Verses 2 & 3 see block lyrics)

know you could_ be wrong.   You say you told_ me That_ you

wan - na hold_ me, But_ you know you're not___ that strong._

I just can't do what I____ done be - fore,____

I just_ can't beg you a - ny - more.___ I'm gon - na let you pass_

And I'll go last.___ Then time will tell___ just

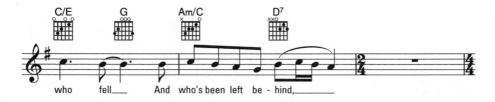

who fell___ And who's been left be - hind,_____

When you go your way and I go mine.

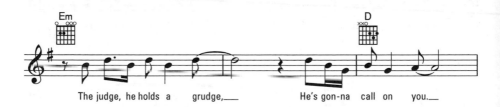

The judge, he holds a grudge,___ He's gon-na call on you.___

But he's bad - ly built And he walks on stilts, Watch out he don't

D.S. al Coda   **⊕ Coda**

fall on you.   mine.

Verse 2:
You say you disturb me
And you don't deserve me
But you know sometimes you lie
You say you're shakin'
And you're always achin'
But you know how hard you try
Sometimes it gets so hard to care
It can't be this way ev'rywhere
And I'm gonna let you pass
Yes, and I'll go last
Then time will tell just who fell
And who's been left behind
When you go your way and I go mine

Verse 3:
You say you're sorry
For tellin' stories
That you know I believe are true
You say ya got some
Other kinda lover
And yes, I believe you do
You say my kisses are not like his
But this time I'm not gonna tell you why that is
I'm just gonna let you pass
Yes, and I'll go last
Then time will tell who fell
And who's been left behind
When you go your way and I go mine

Sad-Eyed Lady Of The Lowlands

Words & Music by Bob Dylan

Moderately slow

1. With your mer - cury mouth_____ in the
(Verses 2-5 see block lyrics)

mis - sion - ar - y times, And your eyes_____ like

smoke_____ and your prayers like rhymes, And your

sil - ver_____ cross, and your voice like

chimes, Oh, who a - mong them do they think could

bu - ry you?___ With your pock - ets well___ pro-

-tect - ed at___ last, And your street - car

vi - sions___ which you place on the grass, And your

flesh like silk, and your face like glass,

Who a - mong them do they think could car - ry you?___

Chorus

Sad - eyed la - dy of___ the low - lands,

Where the sad - eyed   pro - phet   says   that   no   man

comes,   My____   ware - house

eyes,   my   A - ra - bi - an____   drums,

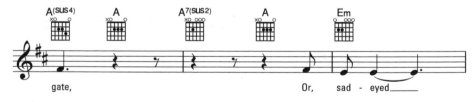

Should   I   leave them   by   your

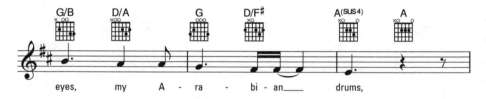

gate,   Or,   sad - eyed____

la - dy,____ should I   wait?_   2. With your

114

Verse 2:
With your sheets like metal and your belt like lace
And your deck of cards missing the jack and the ace
And your basement clothes and your hollow face
Who among them can think he could outguess you?
With your silhouette when the sunlight dims
Into your eyes where the moonlight swims
And your matchbook songs and your gypsy hymns
Who among them would try to impress you?
Chorus:

Verse 3:
The kings of Tyrus with their convict list
Are waiting in line for their geranium kiss
And you wouldn't know it would happen like this
But who among them really wants just to kiss you?
With your childhood flames on your midnight rug
And your Spanish manners and your mother's drugs
And your cowboy mouth and your curfew plugs
Who among them do you think could resist you?
Chorus:

Verse 4:
Oh, the farmers and the businessmen, they all did decide
To show you the dead angels that they used to hide
But why did they pick you to sympathize with their side?
Oh, how could they ever mistake you?
They wished you'd accepted the blame for the farm
But with the sea at your feet and the phony false alarm
And with the child of a hoodlum wrapped up in your arms
How could they ever, ever persuade you?
Chorus:

Verse 5:
With your sheet-metal memory of Cannery Row
And your magazine-husband who one day just had to go
And your gentleness now, which you just can't help but show
Who among them do you think would employ you?
Now you stand with your thief, you're on his parole
With your holy medallion which your fingertips fold
And your saintlike face and your ghostlike soul
Oh, who among them do you think could destroy you?
Chorus:

115

Back To Basics

Dylan's next studio album was *John Wesley Harding* (1968), a collection of pared-down songs made up of old-time Western-style ballads, religious speculations and the atypical 'I'll Be Your Baby Tonight' a country song soon covered by The Byrds. 'All Along The Watchtower' would find its greatest fame with Jimi Hendrix's cover version but the common denominator of this Dylan album seemed to be a new clarity of storytelling. A recent near-death experience on a motorcycle appeared to have made him more focused and spiritually aware, yet he played down this austere album released in the psychedelic age of *Sgt. Pepper*, wanting no singles to be released from it. In the background, however, was a growing collection of songs informally recorded with The Hawks (soon to be The Band) that remained unreleased for years. They're represented here with 'Quinn The Eskimo' (a hit for Manfred Mann) and 'This Wheel's On Fire' (a hit for Julie Driscoll and The Brian Auger Trinity). More odds and ends would soon follow including 'When I Paint My Masterpiece' eventually released in 1971 on a greatest hits compilation...but not until after Dylan's next album, *Nashville Skyline* (1969), a country excursion whose finest moment was perhaps 'Lay, Lady, Lay'. Its successor, the two-disc *Self Portrait* (1970) received almost universally poor reviews. *New Morning*, released the same year, was hailed as something of a return to form with the title track and 'If Not For You' (covered by George Harrison) both standing out. Before that the haunting 'Knockin' On Heaven's Door' emerged from the *Pat Garrett & Billy The Kid* movie soundtrack, another Dylan song perhaps more famous in its cover renditions (by everyone from Eric Clapton to Guns N' Roses) than the original.

I Dreamed I Saw St. Augustine

Words & Music by Bob Dylan

Slowly

Capo fret 3

1. I dreamed I saw St. Au - gu - stine,
(Verses 2 & 3 see block lyrics)

A - live as you or me, Tear - ing through these

quar - ters In the ut - most mi - se - ry, With a

blan - ket un - der - neath his arm And a

coat of so - lid gold, Search - ing for the

ve - ry souls Whom al - rea - dy have been sold. *Play 3 times* 2. "A -

All Along The Watchtower

Verse 2:
"Arise, arise," he cried so loud
In a voice without restraint
"Come out, ye gifted kings and queens
And hear my sad complaint
No martyr is among ye now
Whom you can call your own
So go on your way accordingly
But know you're not alone"

Verse 3:
I dreamed I saw St. Augustine
Alive with fiery breath
And I dreamed I was amongst the ones
That put him out to death
Oh, I awoke in anger
So alone and terrified
I put my fingers against the glass
And bowed my head and cried

All Along The Watchtower

Words & Music by Bob Dylan

Moderately

Capo fret 4

1. "There must be some way out___ of here," said the jok-er to the thief.

"There's too much con - fu - sion, I can't get no re - lief.___

Busi-ness-men,_ they drink my wine, plow - men_ dig my earth,

None of them a - long the line_____ know what an-y of it is worth."___

2. "No rea-son to get ex - cit - ed," the thief, he kind-ly spoke,___

"There are ma-ny here a - mong us who feel that life is but a joke.

But you and I, we've been through that, and this is not our fate,____

So let us not talk false-ly now, The hour is get-ting late."____

3. All a-long the watch tow-er,____ prin-ces kept the view____

While all the wo-men came and went, bare-foot ser-vants, too.____

Out-side_ in the dis-tance a wild-cat did growl,____

Two rid-ers were ap-proach-ing, the wind be-gan to howl.

Drifter's Escape

Words & Music by Bob Dylan

Moderately

1. "Oh,　　help me　　in my weak-
(Verses 2 & 3 see block lyrics)

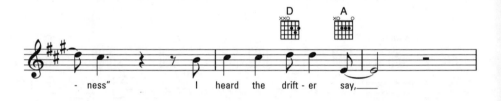

- ness"　　I heard the drift- er say,___

As they car-ried him___ from the court-room　And were tak-

- ing him a - way.___　　"My trip___

___ has- n't been a plea - sant one　And my___

122

_____ time it is - n't long, _____ And I_____

_____ still do not know _____ What is was _____ that I've done wrong." _____

1, 2.   **3.**

_____ 2. Well, the
3. "Oh,

Verse 2:
Well, the judge, he cast his robe aside
A tear came to his eye
"You fail to understand," he said
"Why must you even try?"
Outside the crowd was stirring
You could hear it from the door
Inside, the judge was stepping down
While the jury cried for more

Verse 3:
"Oh, stop that cursed jury"
Cried the attendant and the nurse,
"The trial was bad enough
But this is ten times worse"
Just then a bolt of lightning
Struck the courthouse out of shape
And while ev'rybody knelt to pray
The drifter did escape

I Pity The Poor Immigrant

Words & Music by Bob Dylan

Moderately

Capo fret 5

1. I pi - ty the poor im - mi - grant Who

(Verses 2 & 3 see block lyrics)

wish - es he would -'ve stayed home,

Who us - es all his pow - er to do

ev - il But in the end is al - ways left so a-

- lone. That man whom

with his fin - gers cheats And who lies with

ev - 'ry___ breath,   Who

pas - sion - ate - ly   hates   his   life   And

Play 3 times

like - wise,   fears___ his___   death.___   2. I

Verse 2:
I pity the poor immigrant
Whose strength is spent in vain
Whose heaven is like Ironsides
Whose tears are like rain
Who eats but is not satisfied
Who hears but does not see
Who falls in love with wealth itself
And turns his back on me

Verse 3:
I pity the poor immigrant
Who tramples through the mud
Who fills his mouth with laughing
And who builds his town with blood
Whose visions in the final end
Must shatter like the glass
I pity the poor immigrant
When his gladness comes to pass

I'll Be Your Baby Tonight

Words & Music by Bob Dylan

1. Close your eyes, _____ close the door, ___
(2.) light, _____ shut the shade, ___

You don't have to wor - ry _____ an - y - more. ___
You don't have _____ to be a - fraid. ___

I'll _____ be your _____ ba - by to -

1.

- night. _____ 2. Shut the

2.

Well, that mock - ing - bird's gon - na

Quinn The Eskimo
(The Mighty Quinn)

Words & Music by Bob Dylan

Brightly

Verse

1. Ev - 'ry - bo - dy's build - ing the
(Verses 2 & 3 see block lyrics)

big ships and the boats, Some are build - ing mon - u - ments,

Oth - ers, jot - ting down notes, Ev - 'ry - bo - dy's in des - pair,

Ev - 'ry girl and boy But when Quinn the Es - ki - mo gets here, Ev - 'ry-

-bo - dy's gon - na jump for joy.

Chorus

Come all with - out,

come all with - in, You'll not see no - thing like the might - y Quinn.

128

Come all with-out, come all with-in, You'll not see no-thin' like the

1, 2.

3.

might-y Quinn.＿ might-y Quinn.＿

Verse 2:
I like to do just like the rest, I like my sugar sweet
But guarding fumes and making haste
It ain't my cup of meat
Ev'rybody's 'neath the trees
Feeding pigeons on a limb
But when Quinn the Eskimo gets here
All the pigeons gonna run to him
Chorus:

Verse 3:
A cat's meow and a cow's moo, I can recite 'em all
Just tell me where it hurts yuh, honey
And I'll tell you who to call
Nobody can get no sleep
There's someone on ev'ryone's toes
But when Quinn the Eskimo gets here
Ev'rybody's gonna wanna doze
Chorus:

You Ain't Goin' Nowhere

Words & Music by Bob Dylan

Moderately

1. Clouds so swift___ Rain won't lift___
(Verses 2 & 3 see block lyrics)

Gate won't close___ Rail - ings froze___ Get your mind___

off win - ter - time___ You ain't goin'___ no - where___

Chorus

Whoo - ee!___ Ride me high___ To - mor - row's the day My

bride's gon - na come Oh, oh,___ Are we gon - na fly

130

Verse 2:
I don't care
How many letters they sent
Morning came and morning went
Pick up your money
And pack up your tent
You ain't goin' nowhere
Chorus:

Verse 3:
Buy me a flute
And a gun that shoots
Tailgates and substitutes
Strap yourself
To the tree with roots
You ain't goin' nowhere
Chorus:

This Wheel's On Fire

Words by Bob Dylan
Music by Rick Danko

Slowly

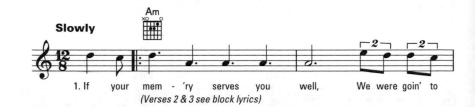

1. If your mem - 'ry serves you well, We were goin' to

(Verses 2 & 3 see block lyrics)

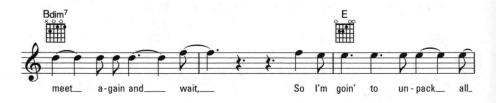

meet___ a-gain and___ wait,___ So I'm goin' to un-pack___ all___

___ my things And sit be-fore it gets too late. No

man___ a - live___ will come to you With an -

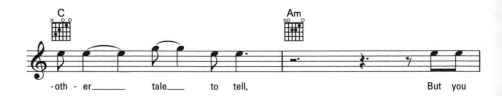

-oth - er___ tale___ to tell, But you

know_____ that we_____ shall meet a - gain,_____ If your

mem - 'ry_____ serves you well.

Chorus This wheel's on fire, Roll - ing down the road,__

Best no - ti - fy my

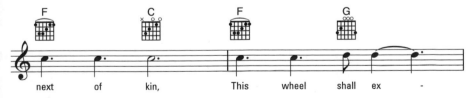

next of kin, This wheel shall ex -

1, 2. A

- plode!_____

3. A

2, 3. If your - plode!_____

133

Verse 2:
If your mem'ry serves you well
I was goin' to confiscate your lace
And wrap it up in a sailor's knot
And hide it in your case
If I knew for sure that it was yours...
But it was oh so hard to tell
But you knew that we would meet again
If your mem'ry serves you well
Chorus:

Verse 3:
If your mem'ry serves you well
You'll remember you're the one
That called on me to call on them
To get you your favors done
And after ev'ry plan had failed
And there was nothing more to tell
You knew that we would meet again
If your mem'ry serves you well
Chorus:

Tears Of Rage

Words & Music by Bob Dylan & Richard Manuel

Slowly

Capo fret 2

We car - ried you____ in our arms____ On
(Verses 2 & 3 see block lyrics)

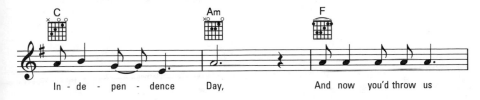

In - de - pen - dence Day, And now you'd throw us

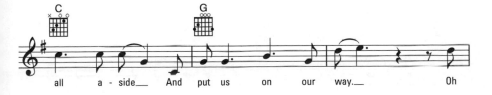

all a - side____ And put us on our way.____ Oh

what dear daugh - ter 'neath the sun_____ Would

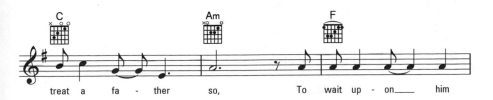

treat a fa - ther so, To wait up - on____ him

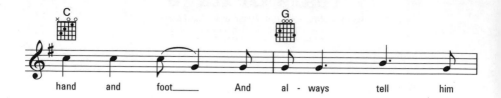

hand and foot_____ And al - ways tell him

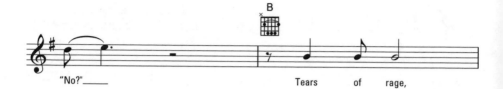

"No?"_____ Tears of rage,

tears of grief,_____ Why must I al - ways

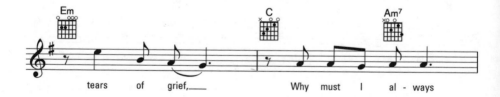

be the thief? Come to me now,___ you know We're

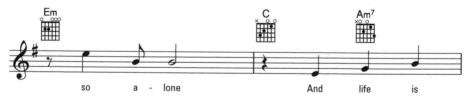

so a - lone And life is

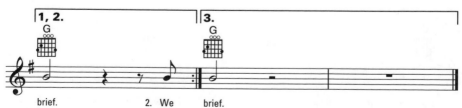

1, 2.   **3.**

brief.   2. We   brief.

Verse 2:
We pointed out the way to go
And scratched your name in sand
Though you just thought it was nothing more
Than a place for you to stand
Now, I want you to know that while we watched
You discover there was no one true
Most ev'rybody really thought
It was a childish thing to do
Tears of rage, tears of grief
Must I always be the thief?
Come to me now, you know
We're so low
And life is brief

Verse 3:
It was all very painless
When you went out to receive
All that false instruction
Which we never could believe
And now the heart is filled with gold
As if It was a purse
But, oh, what kind of love is this
Which goes from bad to worse?
Tears of rage, tears of grief
Must I always be the thief?
Come to me now, you know
We're so low
And life is brief

Lay, Lady, Lay

Words & Music by Bob Dylan

Moderately

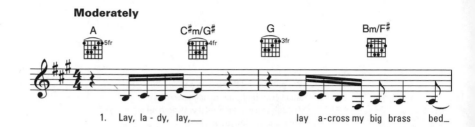

1. Lay, la - dy, lay,___ lay a-cross my big brass bed_

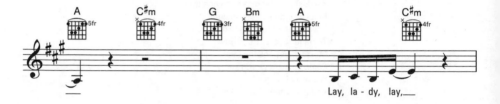

Lay, la - dy, lay,___

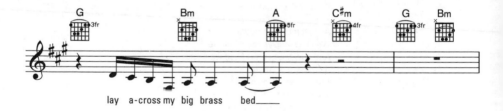

lay a-cross my big brass bed_____

What-ev - er col - ors you have_ in your mind_

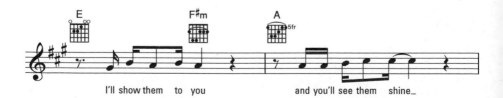

I'll show them to you and you'll see them shine_

138

2. Lay, la - dy, lay,___ lay a-cross my big brass bed___

Stay, la - dy, stay,___

stay with your man___ a - while___

Un - til the break of___ day,___ let me see you make him smile___

His clothes are dir - ty but his___

hands are clean___ And you're the best___ thing that he's

ev - er seen___ 3. Stay, la - dy, stay,___

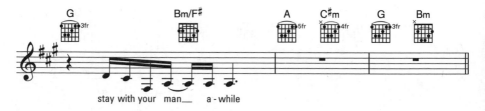

stay with your man___ a - while

Why wait an - y long - er for___ the world to be - gin___

You can have your cake___ and eat it too_____

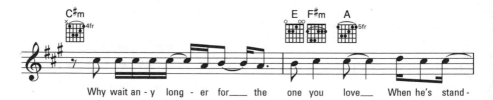

Why wait an - y long - er for____ the one you love___ When he's stand -

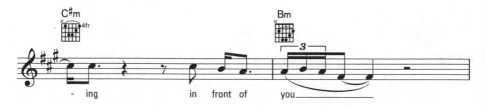

- ing in front of you_____

140

4. Lay, la-dy, lay,— lay a-cross my big brass bed——

Stay, la-dy stay, stay while the night— is still a - head—

I long— to see— you in the

morn-ing light— I long to reach for you in the night—

Stay, la - dy, stay,— stay while the night— is still a - head.—

I Threw It All Away

Words & Music by Bob Dylan

Slowly

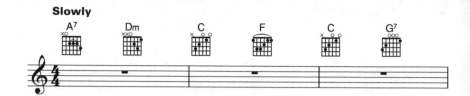

1. I once held her___ in my arms,___

She said she would al - ways stay.___

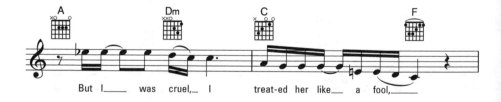

But I___ was cruel, I treat-ed her like___ a fool,___

I threw it all a - way.___

142

2. Once I had moun-tains in the palm of my hand,

And riv - ers that ran__ through__ ev -'ry day.__

I must have been mad,__ I nev - er knew what I had,

Un - til I__ threw it all a - way.__

Love is all there is,__ it makes the world go 'round,__

143

Love and on - ly love,__ it can't be de - nied.

No mat - ter what you think a - bout__ it

You just won't be a - ble to do with - out__ it.

Take a tip__ from one who's tried.__

3. So if you find__ some-one that gives you all of her love,__

Take it to your heart, don't_____ let it stray,_____

For one_____ thing that's cer-tain, You_____ will sure-ly be_____ a-hurt-in',

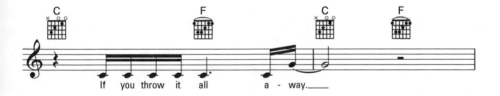

If you throw it all a-way._____

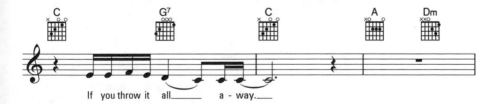

If you throw it all_____ a-way._____

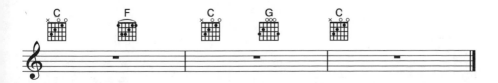

Tonight I'll Be Staying Here With You

Words & Music by Bob Dylan

Moderately slow

1. Throw my tick - et out the win - dow,

Throw my suit - case out there, too,___

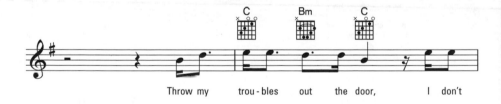

Throw my trou - bles out the door, I don't

need them an - y more 'Cause to - night I'll be stay - ing here with

you.   2. I should have left this town_ this

146

morn - ing But it was more than I could

do. Oh, your

love comes on so strong And I've wait - ed all day long___ For to -

-night when I'll be stay - ing here with you.

Is it real - ly an - y won - der

The love that a strang - er might re - ceive.

147

You cast your spell and I went un - der

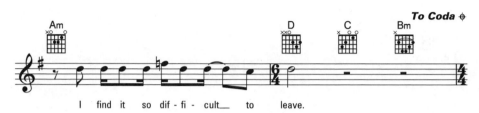

To Coda

I find it so dif - fi - cult___ to leave.

N.C.

3. I can hear that whis - tle blow - in',

I see that sta - tion - mas - ter,

too   If there's a

poor boy on the street, Then let him have my seat 'Cause to -

- night   I'll   be   stay - ing   here   with   you._____

D.S. al Coda
(instrumental)

Coda

4. Throw my   tick - et   out____   the   win - dow,

Throw my   suit - case   out____   there,

too   Throw   my

trou - bles   out   the   door,   I   don't   need   them   a - ny   more   'Cause to -

- night   I'll   be   stay - ing   here   with   you.

149

If Not For You

Words & Music by Bob Dylan

Moderately bright

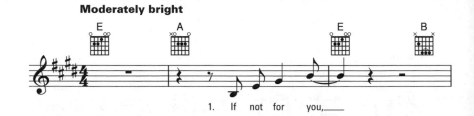

1. If not for you,___

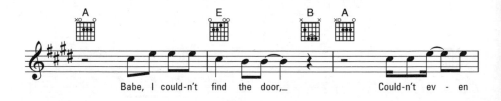

Babe, I could-n't find the door,___ Could-n't ev - en

ooo tho floor___ I'd he sad and blue,___

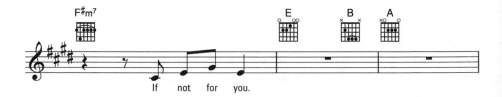

If not for you.

2. If not for you,___

150

Babe, I'd___ lay a-wake all night,___ Wait for the

morn - in' light___ to shine in through,___

But it would not be new,___ If not for you.

If not for you My sky would fall, Rain would ga-ther

too.___ With-out your love I'd be no-where at all, I'd

be lost if not for you, And you know it's true.

If not for you My sky would fall, Rain would ga-ther too.

— With-out your love I'd be no-where at all, Oh!—

— What would I___ do___ If not___ for you._____

3. If not for you,____

Win-ter would have no spring, Could-n't hear the

ro - bin sing,__ I just would-n't have a clue,__

A - ny - way it would - n't ring true,_____

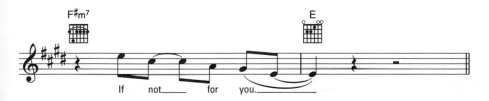

If not__ for you._____

Repeat to fade

If not for__ you._____

153

Watching The River Flow

Words & Music by Bob Dylan

Moderate blues

1. What's the mat - ter with me,___ I don't have

(Verse 2 see block lyrics)

much to say,___

Day-light sneak-in' through the win-dow and I'm still in this all -

- night ca - fé. Walk-in' to and fro___ be-neath the

moon Out to where the trucks are___ roll - in' slow,

To sit down on___ this bank of sand___

And watch the riv - er flow.

3. Peo - ple dis a - gree - ing on all just a - bout ev - 'ry- thing,_ yeah,
(Verse 4 see block lyrics)

Makes you stop and all___ won - der why.___ Why

on - ly yes-ter-day I saw some-bo - dy on the street Who just___ could-n't help but

cry. Oh,___ this ol' ri - ver keeps on roll - in'

though, No mat - ter what gets in the way and which way the

155

Verse 2:
Wish I was back in the city
Instead of this old bank of sand
With the sun beating down over the chimney tops
And the one I love so close at hand
If I had wings and I could fly
I know where I would go
But right now I'll just sit here so contentedly
And watch the river flow

Verse 4:
People disagreeing everywhere you look
Makes you wanna stop and read a book
Why only yesterday I saw somebody on the street
That was really shook
But this ol' river keeps on rollin', though
No matter what gets in the way and which way the wind does blow
And as long as it does I'll just sit here
And watch the river flow

I Shall Be Released

Words & Music by Bob Dylan

Slowly

Capo fret 2

1. They say ev -'ry-thing can be re - placed,_____
2. They say ev -'ry man___ needs pro - tec - tion,____

Yet ev -'ry dis-tance is not near._____ So I re-mem-ber ev -'ry
They say___ ev -'ry man must fall._____ Yet I swear I___ see my re-

face_____ Of ev -'ry man___ who put me
- flec - tion_____ Some place so high___ a - bove this

here._____ } I see my light come shin - ing
wall._____ }

From the west_ un - to the east._____ An - y day now,

an - y day now, I shall be re - leased._____

I shall be re - leased._____ 3. Stand-ing next to me in this lone - ly

crowd,_____ Is a man who swears he's not to blame._____

All day long I hear him shout_____ so loud,

Cry - ing out that he was framed._____

I shall be re - leased._____

159

New Morning

Words & Music by Bob Dylan

Moderately

1. Can't you hear_ that_ roost-er crow - in'?_____
(Verse 2 see block lyrics)

Rab - bit run - nin' down a - cross the road

Un - der - neath the bridge_____ where the wa - ter flowed_____ through_____

So hap - py just to

see you smile_____ Un - der - neath the sky_____ of blue On this new_

_ morn - ing,_____ new morn - ing On this

new   morn- ing_____ with   you.

The   night_ passed   a - way   so_____   quick - ly_____

It   al - ways   does____   when   you're_   with_

___ me._____

3. Can't   you   feel   that

sun_____   a - shin - in'?_____

Ground-hog run-nin'   by the coun-try   stream_   This must be the day that

all of my___ dreams come true___

So hap - py just to be a - live_____ Un - der - neath_

___ the sky___ of blue On this new___

morn - ing,_____ new morn - ing On this

new morn - ing with you.

Repeat to fade

New morn - ing..._____

Verse 2:
Can't you hear that motor turnin'?
Automobile comin' into style
Comin' down the road for a country mile or two
So happy just to see you smile
Underneath the sky of blue
On this new morning, new morning
On this new morning with you

162

When I Paint My Masterpiece

Words & Music by Bob Dylan

Moderately slow

1. Oh, the streets of Rome are filled with rub-ble,— An-cient foot-
(Verse 2 see block lyrics)

-prints— are ev - 'ry - where.— You can

al - most think— that you're see - in' dou - ble— On a

cold, dark night— on the Spa - nish Stairs.—

Got to hur-ry on back— to my ho - tel room, Where I've

got me a date with Bot - ti - cel - li's niece. She

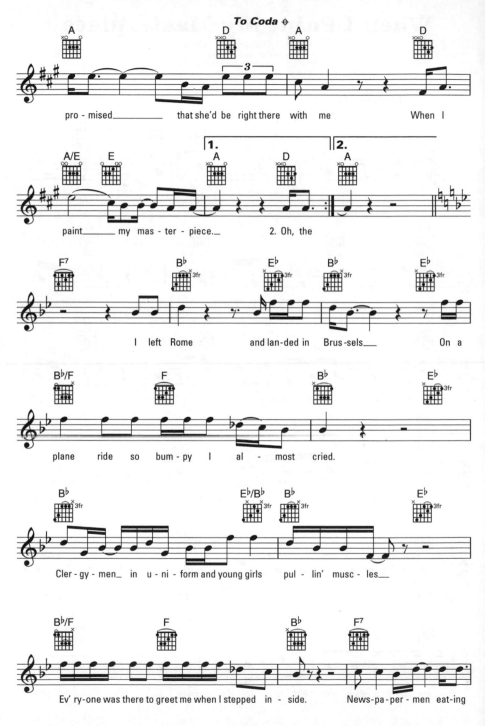

pro - mised_____ that she'd be right there with me   When I

paint_____ my mas - ter - piece.___   2. Oh, the

I left Rome   and lan - ded in Brus - sels___   On a

plane   ride   so   bum - py   I   al - most   cried.

Cler - gy - men_ in u - ni - form and young girls   pul - lin' musc - les__

Ev' ry-one was there to greet me when I stepped in - side.   News-pa-per - men eating

164

Verse 2:
Oh, the hours I've spent inside the Coliseum
Dodging lions and wastin' time
Oh, those mighty kings of the jungle, I could hardly stand to see 'em
Yes, it sure has been a long, hard climb
Train wheels runnin' through the back of my memory
When I ran on the hilltop following a pack of wild geese
Someday, everything is gonna be smooth like a rhapsody
When I paint my masterpiece

Knockin' On Heaven's Door

Words & Music by Bob Dylan

Slowly

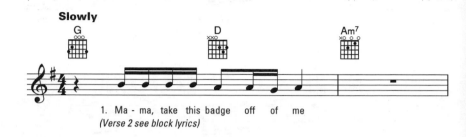

1. Ma - ma, take this badge off of me
(Verse 2 see block lyrics)

I can't use__ it an - y - more.__

It's get - tin' dark, too dark for me to see

I feel like I'm knock - in' on heav - en's door.__

Knock, knock, knock - in' on heav - en's door.__

Verse 2:
Mama, put my guns in the ground
I can't shoot them any more
That long black cloud is comin' down
I feel like I'm knockin' on heaven's door

Knock, knock, knockin' on heaven's door
Knock, knock, knockin' on heaven's door
Knock, knock, knockin' on heaven's door
Knock, knock, knockin' on heaven's door

Forever Young

Words & Music by Bob Dylan

Slowly

1. May God bless and keep you al - ways,___ May your

wish-es all come true,___ May you al-ways do for oth - ers And let

oth-ers do___ for you.___ May you

build a lad-der to the stars___ And climb on ev-'ry rung,___ May you stay

for - ev - er young,___

For - ev - er young,_____ for -

168

-ev-er young,_____ May_ you_ stay_____

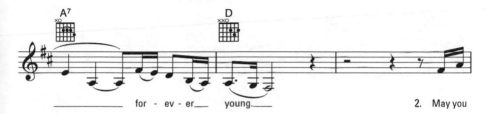

_____ for - ev - er_ young._ 2. May you

grow up to be right-eous, May you grow up to be true,_____ May you

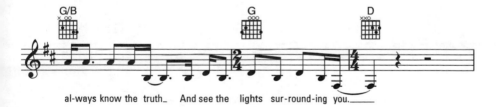

al-ways know the truth_ And see the lights sur-round-ing you._____

May you al-ways be cou-ra - geous,_Stand up-right and be strong,_ May you

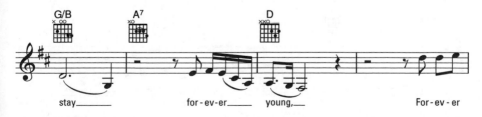

stay_____ for - ev-er_____ young,_ For-ev - er

169

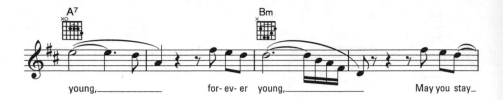

young,_____ for- ev- er young,_____ May you stay_

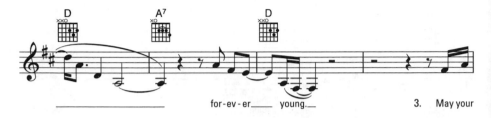

_____ for- ev- er_____ young._ 3. May your

hands al-ways be bu-sy, May your feet al - ways be swift, May you

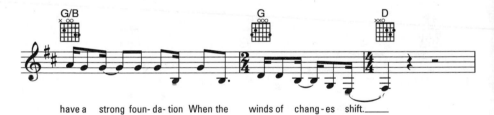

have a strong foun- da- tion When the winds of chang- es shift._____

May your heart al-ways be joy- ful, May your song al - ways be sung, May you

stay_____ for- ev - er young,_____

170

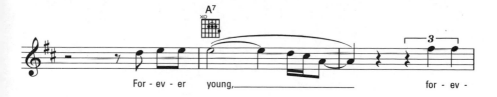

For - ev - er young,_____ for - ev -

- er young,_____ May you stay____

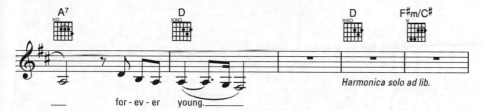

Harmonica solo ad lib.

____ for - ev - er young.____

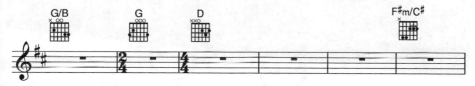

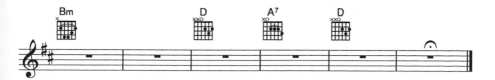

171

Hitting The High Spots

Upon its release *Blood On The Tracks* immediately became the new benchmark for Dylan's work. This collection features seven tracks from a 1975 masterpiece which was so good that it left even the most loyal Dylan fans wondering what could possibly follow it. 'Tangled Up In Blue' and 'Simple Twist Of Fate' set the bar pretty high. Dylan responded with *Desire* in 1976, a sometimes painfully honest album that included a old-style social injustice broadside ('Hurricane'), a Mexican gunfighter ballad ('Romance In Durango') and a Western grave-robbing narrative ('Isis'). A superb album, it was very well received and sold well.

Tangled Up In Blue

Words & Music by Bob Dylan

Moderately

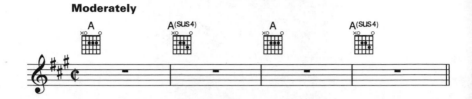

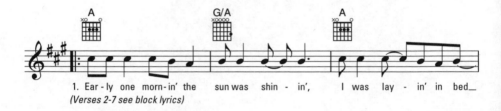

1. Ear - ly one morn - in' the sun was shin - in', I was lay - in' in bed
(Verses 2-7 see block lyrics)

Won d'rin' if___ she'd changed at all___ If her hair___

___ was still red. Her folks, they said our lives___

___ to - geth - er Sure was gon - na be rough___ They

nev-er did like__ Ma-ma's home-made dress, Pa-pa's bank-book was-n't big e-

- nough. And I was stand-in' on the side of the road__

Rain fall-in' on my shoes__ Head-ing out for the East_

__ Coast Lord knows I've paid some dues get-tin' through,__

Tan - gled up in blue.

1-6.

7.

175

Verse 2:
She was married when we first met
Soon to be divorced
I helped her out of a jam, I guess
But I used a little too much force
We drove that car as far as we could
Abandoned it out West
Split up on a dark sad night
Both agreeing it was best
She turned around to look at me
As I was walkin' away
I heard her say over my shoulder
"We'll meet again someday on the avenue"
Tangled up in blue

Verse 3:
I had a job in the great north woods
Working as a cook for a spell
But I never did like it all that much
And one day the ax just fell
So I drifted down to New Orleans
Where I happened to be employed
Workin' for a while on a fishin' boat
Right outside of Delacroix
But all the while I was alone
The past was close behind
I seen a lot of women
But she never escaped my mind, and I just grew
Tangled up in blue

Verse 4:
She was workin' in a topless place
And I stopped in for a beer
I just kept lookin' at the side of her face
In the spotlight so clear
And later on as the crowd thinned out
I's just about to do the same
She was standing there in back of my chair
Said to me, "Don't I know your name?"
I muttered somethin' underneath my breath
She studied the lines on my face
I must admit I felt a little uneasy
When she bent down to tie the laces of my shoe
Tangled up in blue

Verse 5:
She lit a burner on the stove and offered me a pipe
"I thought you'd never say hello," she said
"You look like the silent type"
Then she opened up a book of poems
And handed it to me
Written by an Italian poet
From the thirteenth century
And every one of them words rang true
And glowed like burnin' coal
Pourin' off of every page
Like it was written in my soul from me to you
Tangled up in blue

Verse 6:
I lived with them on Montague Street
In a basement down the stairs
There was music in the cafés at night
And revolution in the air
Then he started into dealing with slaves
And something inside of him died
She had to sell everything she owned
And froze up inside
And when finally the bottom fell out
I became withdrawn
The only thing I knew how to do
Was to keep on keepin' on like a bird that flew
Tangled up in blue

Verse 7:
So now I'm goin' back again
I got to get to her somehow
All the people we used to know
They're an illusion to me now
Some are mathematicians
Some are carpenter's wives
Don't know how it all got started
I don't know what they're doin' with their lives
But me, I'm still on the road
Headin' for another joint
We always did feel the same
We just saw it from a different point of view
Tangled up in blue

Simple Twist Of Fate

Words & Music by Bob Dylan

1. They sat to - geth - er in the park
(Verses 2 & 3 see block lyrics)

As the eve-ning sky___ grew dark, She looked at him and he felt a

spark tin-gle to___ his bones.___ 'Twas then he felt a - lone___

___ and wished___ that he'd gone straight_____ And

watched out_____ for a sim-ple twist of fate.___

They walked a - long by the old_____ ca - nal_____

F#m/C#

A lit - tle con - fused, I re - mem - ber well

D/C   D⁷   G

And stopped in - to a strange_ ho - tel_ with a ne - on burn - in' bright._

Gm

_ He felt the heat_ of the night_

D   F#m   G   D

hit him like a freight_____ train_ Mov - ing_____ with a sim-

1, 2.   **3.**

G/A   D   D

- ple twist_ of fate._

178

Verse 2:
A saxophone someplace far off played
As she was walkin' by the arcade
As the light bust through a beat-up shade where he was wakin' up
She dropped a coin into the cup of a blind man at the gate
And forgot about a simple twist of fate

He woke up, the room was bare
He didn't see her anywhere
He told himself he didn't care, pushed the window open wide
Felt an emptiness inside to which he just could not relate
Brought on by a simple twist of fate

Verse 3:
He hears the ticking of the clocks
And walks along with a parrot that talks
Hunts her down by the waterfront docks where the sailors all come in
Maybe she'll pick him out again, how long must he wait
Once more for a simple twist of fate

People tell me it's a sin
To know and feel too much within
I still believe she was my twin, but I lost the ring
She was born in spring, but I was born too late
Blame it on a simple twist of fate

You're A Big Girl Now

Words & Music by Bob Dylan

Moderately slow

1. Our con-ver-sa-tion___ was short and sweet___ It near-ly swept me___ off-a my feet.___ And I'm back in the rain,___ oh,___ oh, And you are on dry land.___ ___ You made it there___ some - - how You're a big___ girl now.

1-4. **5.** **D.C.** *Instrumental to fade*

180

Verse 2:

Bird on the horizon, sittin' on a fence
He's singin' his song for me at his own expense
And I'm just like that bird, oh, oh
Singin' just for you
I hope that you can hear
Hear me singin' through these tears

Verse 3:

Time is a jet plane, it moves too fast
Oh, but what a shame if all we've shared can't last
I can change, I swear, oh, oh
See what you can do
I can make it through
You can make it too

Verse 4:

Love is so simple, to quote a phrase
You've known it all the time, I'm learnin' it these days
Oh, I know where I can find you, oh, oh
In somebody's room
It's a price I have to pay
You're a big girl all the way

Verse 5:

A change in the weather is known to be extreme
But what's the sense of changing horses in midstream?
I'm going out of my mind, oh, oh
With a pain that stops and starts
Like a corkscrew to my heart
Ever since we've been apart

Idiot Wind

Words & Music by Bob Dylan

Slowly

1. Some - one's got it in_____ for me, they're___
(Verses 2-4 see block lyrics)

____ plant - ing___ sto - ries___ in the___ press

Who - ev - er it is___ I wish they'd cut it out but when they will_____ I can on - ly

guess.___ They say I shot a man__ named Gray__ and

took his wife__ to I - ta - ly,___ She in - her - it - ed a mil - lion bucks and

when she died__ it came to me.__ I can't help it____ if I'm luck - y.___

Peo-ple see me all the time___ and they just can't re-mem - ber how to

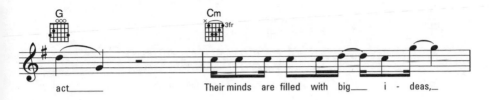

act_____ Their minds are filled with big___ i - deas,___

i - ma - ges_____ and dis-tor-ted facts._____

Ev-en you,___ yes-ter-day___ you had to ask___ me where___ it was___ at, I

could-n't be- lieve af-ter all these years,___ you did-n't know me bet-ter than that___

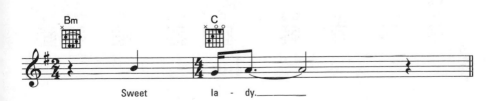

Sweet la - dy._____

183

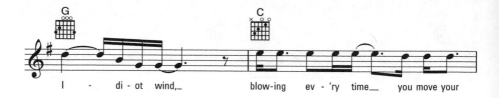

I - di - ot wind,___ blow-ing ev - 'ry time___ you move your

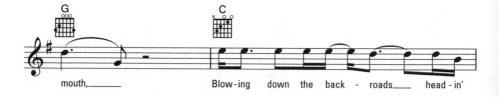

mouth,_____ Blow-ing down the back - roads___ head - in'

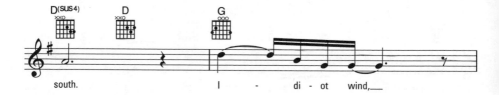

south. I - di - ot wind,___

blow-ing ev - 'ry time___ you move___ your teeth,_____ You're an

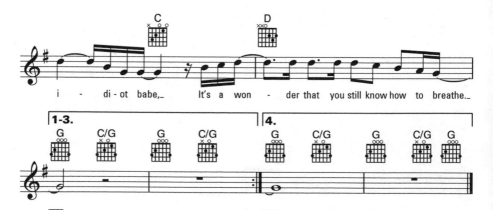

i - di - ot babe,__ It's a won - der that you still know how to breathe._

1-3. G C/G G C/G **4.** G C/G G C/G G

Verse: 2

I ran into the fortune-teller, who said beware of lightning that might strike
I haven't known peace and quiet for so long I can't remember what it's like
There's a lone soldier on the cross, smoke pourin' out of a boxcar door
You didn't know it, you didn't think it could be done, in the final end he won the wars
After losin' every battle

I woke up on the roadside, daydreamin' 'bout the way things sometimes are
Visions of your chestnut mare shoot through my head and are makin' me see stars
You hurt the ones that I love best and cover up the truth with lies
One day you'll be in the ditch, flies buzzin' around your eyes
Blood on your saddle

Idiot wind, blowing through the flowers on your tomb
Blowing through the curtains in your room
Idiot wind, blowing every time you move your teeth
You're an idiot, babe
It's a wonder that you still know how to breathe

Verse 3:

It was gravity which pulled us down and destiny which broke us apart
You tamed the lion in my cage but it just wasn't enough to change my heart
Now everything's a little upside down, as a matter of fact the wheels have stopped
What's good is bad, what's bad is good, you'll find out when you reach the top
You're on the bottom

I noticed at the ceremony, your corrupt ways had finally made you blind
I can't remember your face anymore, your mouth has changed, your eyes don't look into mine
The priest wore black on the seventh day and sat stone-faced while the building burned
I waited for you on the running boards, near the cypress trees, while the springtime turned
Slowly into Autumn

Idiot wind, blowing like a circle around my skull
From the Grand Coulee Dam to the Capitol
Idiot wind, blowing every time you move your teeth
You're an idiot, babe
It's a wonder that you still know how to breathe

Verse 4:

I can't feel you anymore, I can't even touch the books you've read
Every time I crawl past your door, I been wishin' I was somebody else instead
Down the highway, down the tracks, down the road to ecstasy
I followed you beneath the stars, hounded by your memory
And all your ragin' glory

I been double-crossed now for the very last time and now I'm finally free
I kissed goodbye the howling beast on the borderline which separated you from me
You'll never know the hurt I suffered nor the pain I rise above
And I'll never know the same about you, your holiness or your kind of love
And it makes me feel so sorry

Idiot wind, blowing through the buttons of our coats
Blowing through the letters that we wrote
Idiot wind, blowing through the dust upon our shelves
We're idiots, babe
It's a wonder we can even feed ourselves

If You See Her, Say Hello

Words & Music by Bob Dylan

Moderately slow

1. If you see__ her, say__ hel-lo, she
(Verses 2-5 see block lyrics)

might be in__ Tan - gier__ She left here__ last ear-

- ly Spring,__ is liv - in' there,__ I hear__

__ Say for me__ that I'm__

__ all right__ though things get kind of slow__ She might think__

186

that I've for - got - ten her, don't

Play 5 times

tell her it is - n't so._____

Verse 2:
We had a falling-out, like lovers often will
And to think of how she left that night, it still brings me a chill
And though our separation, it pierced me to the heart
She still lives inside of me, we've never been apart

Verse 3:
If you get close to her, kiss her once for me
I always have respected her for busting out and gettin' free
Oh, whatever makes her happy, I won't stand in the way
Though the bitter taste still lingers on from the night I tried to make her stay

Verse 4:
I see a lot of people as I make the rounds
And I hear her name here and there as I go from town to town
And I've never gotten used to it, I've just learned to turn it off
Either I'm too sensitive or else I'm gettin' soft

Verse 5:
Sundown, yellow moon, I replay the past
I know every scene by heart, they all went by so fast
If she's passin' back this way, I'm not that hard to find
Tell her she can look me up if she's got the time

You're Gonna Make Me Lonesome When You Go

Words & Music by Bob Dylan

Moderately fast

E   Emaj7   A/E

1. I've seen love go   by my door   It's nev-er been_ this close be-fore_
(Verses 2 & 3 see block lyrics)

E   Emaj7   B¹¹

Nev-er been so ea-sy   or so slow.   Been

E   Emaj7   A/E

shoot-ing in___ the dark too long_ When some-thin's not right it's wrong

E   B¹¹   E

Play 3 times

Yer gon - na make me lone - some_ when you go.

B¹¹   E

Flow-ers on the hill - side, bloom-in' cra-zy,_____
(2° see block lyrics)

188

Crick-ets talk-in' back___ and forth_ in rhyme,

Blue riv-er run — nin' slow and la - zy,

I could stay with you for-ev - er And nev-er re-al-ize the time.

Verse

4. Si - tu-a - tions have end-ed sad,_ Re - la-tion-ships_ have all___ been bad.__
(Verse 5 see block lyrics)

Mine-'ve been like Ver-laine's___ and Rim - baud.___ But

there's no way I can___ com-pare   All those scenes to this af - fair,___

Yer gon - na make me lone - some when you go.___

Verse 2:
Dragon clouds so high above
I've only known careless love
It's always hit me from below
This time around it's more correct
Right on target, so direct
Yer gonna make me lonesome when you go

Verse 3:
Purple clover, Queen Anne's lace
Crimson hair across your face
You could make me cry if you don't know
Can't remember what I was thinking of
You might be spoilin' me too much, love
Yer gonna make me lonesome when you go

Yer gonna make me wonder what I'm doin'
Stayin' far behind without you
Yer gonna make me wonder what I'm sayin'
Yer gonna make me give myself a good talkin' to

Verse 5:
I'll look for you in old Honolulu
San Francisco, Ashtabula
Yer gonna have to leave me now, I know
But I'll see you in the sky above
In the tall grass, in the ones I love
Yer gonna make me lonesome when you go

Shelter From The Storm

Words & Music by Bob Dylan

1.'Twas in an-oth-er life - time, one of toil__ and blood__ When
(Verses 2-5 see block lyrics)

black-ness was a vir - tue and the road was full of mud____

I came in from__ the wil - der-ness a crea-ture void__ of form.

__ "Come in," she said "I'll give you shel-ter from__ the

storm." And

191

if I pass__ this way a-gain   you can rest__ as-sured___   I'll

al - ways do my best___ for her,   on that I give___ my word_

___   In a world of steel - eyed death, and men__ who are

fight-ing   to be   warm.___   "Come in," she said "I'll give_

___ you   shel-ter from__ the storm."

1-4.

5.

2. Not a

Verse 2:
Not a word was spoke between us, there was little risk involved
Everything up to that point had been left unresolved
Try imagining a place where it's always safe and warm
"Come in,"she said, "I'll give you shelter from the storm"
I was burned out from exhaustion, buried in the hail
Poisoned in the bushes an' blown out on the trail
Hunted like a crocodile, ravaged in the corn
"Come in,"she said, "I'll give you shelter from the storm"

Verse 3:
Suddenly I turned around and she was standin' there
With silver bracelets on her wrists and flowers in her hair
She walked up to me so gracefully and took my crown of thorns
"Come in,"she said, "I'll give you shelter from the storm"
Now there's a wall between us, somethin' there's been lost
I took too much for granted, got my signals crossed
Just to think that it all began on a long-forgotten morn
"Come in,"she said, "I'll give you shelter from the storm"

Verse 4:
Well, the deputy walks on hard nails and the preacher rides a mount
But nothing really matters much, it's doom alone that counts
And the one-eyed undertaker, he blows a futile horn
"Come in,"she said, "I'll give you shelter from the storm"
I've heard newborn babies wailin' like a mournin' dove
And old men with broken teeth stranded without love
Do I understand your question, man, is it hopeless and forlorn?
"Come in,"she said, "I'll give you shelter from the storm"

Verse 5:
In a little hilltop village they gambled for my clothes
I bargained for salvation an' they gave me a lethal dose
I offered up my innocence and got repaid with scorn
"Come in,"she said, "I'll give you shelter from the storm"
Well, I'm livin' in a foreign country but I'm bound to cross the line
Beauty walks a razor's edge, someday I'll make it mine
If I could only turn back the clock to when God and her were born
"Come in,"she said, "I'll give you shelter from the storm"

Hurricane

Words & Music by Bob Dylan & Jacques Levy

Moderately

1. Pis - tol shots ring out in the bar - room night___
(Verses 2-11 see block lyrics)

En - ter Pat - ty Val - en - tine from the up - per hall.___

She sees the bar - tend - er in a pool of blood,___

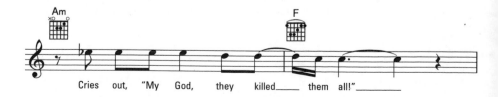

Cries out, "My God, they killed___ them all!"___

194

Here comes the sto - ry of the Hur - ri - cane,

The man the au - tho - ri - ties came to blame

For some - thin' that he nev - er done.

Put in a pri - son cell, but one time he could - a been

The cham - pi - on of the world.

1-10.

11.   D.S.
(Instrumental to fade)

195

Verse 2:
Three bodies lyin' there does Patty see
And another man named Bello, movin' around mysteriously
"I didn't do it," he says, and he throws up his hands
"I was only robbin' the register, I hope you understand
I saw them leavin'," he says, and he stops
"One of us had better call up the cops"
And so Patty calls the cops
And they arrive on the scene with their red lights flashin'
In the hot New Jersey night

Verse 3:
Meanwhile, far away in another part of town
Rubin Carter and a couple of friends are drivin' around
Number one contender for the middleweight crown
Had no idea what kinda shit was about to go down
When a cop pulled him over to the side of the road
Just like the time before and the time before that
In Paterson that's just the way things go
If you're black you might as well not show up on the street
'Less you wanna draw the heat

Verse 4:
 Alfred Bello had a partner and he had a rap for the cops
Him and Arthur Dexter Bradley were just out prowlin' around
He said, "I saw two men runnin' out, they looked like middleweights
They jumped into a white car with out-of-state plates"
And Miss Patty Valentine just nodded her head
Cop said, "Wait a minute, boys, this one's not dead"
So they took him to the infirmary
And though this man could hardly see
They told him that he could identify the guilty men

Verse 5:
Four in the mornin' and they haul Rubin in
Take him to the hospital and they bring him upstairs
The wounded man looks up through his one dyin' eye
Says, "Wha'd you bring him in here for? He ain't the guy!"
Yes, here's the story of the Hurricane
The man the authorities came to blame
For somethin' that he never done
Put in a prison cell, but one time he could-a been
The champion of the world

Verse 6:
Four months later, the ghettos are in flame
Rubin's in South America, fightin' for his name
While Arthur Dexter Bradley's still in the robbery game
And the cops are puttin' the screws to him, lookin' for somebody to blame
"Remember that murder that happened in a bar?"
"Remember you said you saw the getaway car?"
"You think you'd like to play ball with the law?"
"Think it might-a been that fighter that you saw runnin' that night?"
"Don't forget that you are white"

Verse 7:
Arthur Dexter Bradley said, "I'm really not sure"
Cops said, "A poor boy like you could use a break
We got you for the motel job and we're talkin' to your friend Bello
Now you don't wanta have to go back to jail, be a nice fellow
You'll be doin' society a favor
That sonofabitch is brave and gettin' braver
We want to put his ass in stir
We want to pin this triple murder on him
He ain't no Gentleman Jim"

Verse 8:
Rubin could take a man out with just one punch
But he never did like to talk about it all that much
It's my work, he'd say, and I do it for pay
And when it's over I'd just as soon go on my way
Up to some paradise
Where the trout streams flow and the air is nice
And ride a horse along a trail
But then they took him to the jailhouse
Where they try to turn a man into a mouse

Verse 9:
All of Rubin's cards were marked in advance
The trial was a pig-circus, he never had a chance
The judge made Rubin's witnesses drunkards from the slums
To the white folks who watched he was a revolutionary bum
And to the black folks he was just a crazy nigger
No one doubted that he pulled the trigger
And though they could not produce the gun
The D.A. said he was the one who did the deed
And the all-white jury agreed

Verse 10:
Rubin Carter was falsely tried.
The crime was murder "one," guess who testified?
Bello and Bradley and they both baldly lied
And the newspapers, they all went along for the ride
How can the life of such a man
Be in the palm of some fool's hand?
To see him obviously framed
Couldn't help but make me feel ashamed to live in a land
Where justice is a game

Verse 11:
Now all the criminals in their coats and their ties
Are free to drink martinis and watch the sun rise
While Rubin sits like Buddha in a ten-foot cell
An innocent man in a living hell
That's the story of the Hurricane
But it won't be over till they clear his name
And give him back the time he's done
Put in a prison cell, but one time he could-a been
The champion of the world

One More Cup Of Coffee
(Valley Below)

Words & Music by Bob Dylan

Slowly

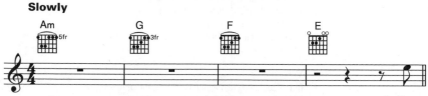

1. Your

breath is sweet__ Your eyes are like_____ two jewels in the sky.__

(Verses 2 & 3 see block lyrics)

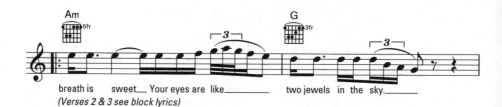

Your back is straight, your hair__ Is smooth__ On the pil-low where you lie.__

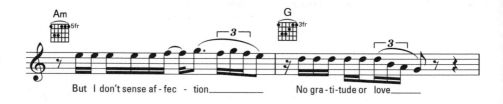

But I don't sense af - fec - tion_____ No gra-ti-tude or love_____

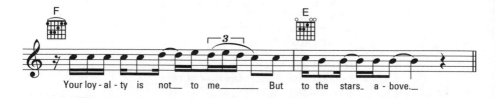

Your loy - al - ty is not__ to me_____ But to the stars__ a - bove.__

198

Chorus

One more cup of cof-fee for the road,___

One more cup of cof-fee 'fore I go___ To the val-ley be-low.___

1, 2. | **3.**

2, 3. Your

Verse 2:
Your daddy he's an outlaw
And a wanderer by trade
He'll teach you how to pick and choose
And how to throw the blade
He oversees his kingdom
So no stranger does intrude
His voice it trembles as he calls out
For another plate of food
Chorus:

Verse 3:
Your sister sees the future
Like your mama and yourself
You've never learned to read or write
There's no books upon your shelf
And your pleasure knows no limits
Your voice is like a meadowlark
But your heart is like an ocean
Mysterious and dark
Chorus:

Oh, Sister

Words by Bob Dylan & Jacques Levy
Music by Bob Dylan

Slowly

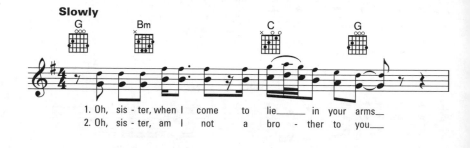

1. Oh, sis - ter, when I come to lie_____ in your arms__
2. Oh, sis - ter, am I not a bro - ther to you___

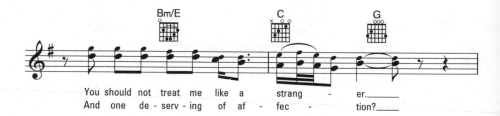

You should not treat me like a strang - er._____
And one de - serv - ing of af - fec - tion?____

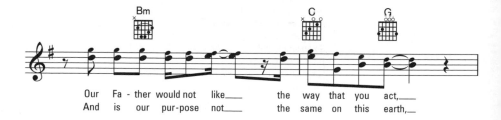

Our Fa - ther would not like____ the way that you act,____
And is our pur-pose not____ the same on this earth,___

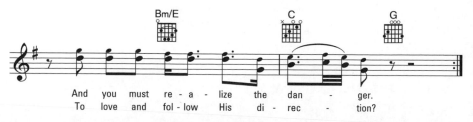

And you must re - a - lize the dan - ger.
To love and fol - low His di - rec - tion?

We grew up to-geth-er from the cra-dle to the grave___ We

died and were re-born And then mys-te-ri-ous-ly saved.___

3. Oh, sis-ter, when I come to knock on your door,___

Don't turn a-way, you'll cre-ate sor-row.___

Time is an o-cean but it ends at the shore___

You may not see me to-mor-row.

Isis

Words by Bob Dylan & Jacques Levy
Music by Bob Dylan

Moderately

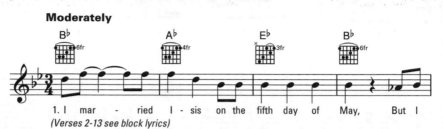

1. I mar - ried I - sis on the fifth day of May, But I
(Verses 2-13 see block lyrics)

could not____ hold on to her____ ve - ry long.____ So I

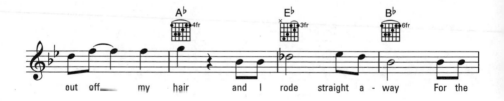

out off____ my hair and I rode straight a - way For the

wild un - known coun - try____ where I could not____ go wrong.

1-12.   13.

2. I

Verse 2:
I came to a high place of darkness and light
The dividing line ran through the center of town
I hitched up my pony to a post on the right
Went in to a laundry to wash my clothes down

Verse 3:
A man in the corner approached me for a match
I knew right away he was not ordinary
He said, "Are you lookin' for somethin' easy to catch?"
I said, "I got no money." He said, "That ain't necessary"

Verse 4
We set out that night for the cold in the North
I gave him my blanket, he gave me his word
I said, "Where are we goin'?" He said we'd be back by the fourth
I said, "That's the best news that I've ever heard"

Verse 5:
I was thinkin' about turquoise, I was thinkin' about gold
I was thinkin' about diamonds and the world's biggest necklace
As we rode through the canyons, through the devilish cold
I was thinkin' about Isis, how she thought I was so reckless

Verse 6:
How she told me that one day we would meet up again
And things would be different the next time we wed
If I only could hang on and just be her friend
I still can't remember all the best things she said

Verse 7:
We came to the pyramids all embedded in ice
He said, "There's a body I'm tryin' to find
If I carry it out it'll bring a good price"
'Twas then that I knew what he had on his mind

Verse 8:
The wind it was howlin' and the snow was outrageous
We chopped through the night and we chopped through the dawn
When he died I was hopin' that it wasn't contagious
But I made up my mind that I had to go on

Verse 9:
I broke into the tomb, but the casket was empty
There was no jewels, no nothin', I felt I'd been had
When I saw that my partner was just bein' friendly
When I took up his offer I must-a been mad

Verse 10:
I picked up his body and I dragged him inside
Threw him down in the hole and I put back the cover
I said a quick prayer and I felt satisfied
Then I rode back to find Isis just to tell her I love her

Verse 11:
She was there in the meadow where the creek used to rise
Blinded by sleep and in need of a bed
I came in from the East with the sun in my eyes
I cursed her one time then I rode on ahead

Verse 12:
She said, "Where ya been?" I said, "No place special"
She said, "You look different." I said, "Well, not quite"
She said, "You been gone." I said, "That's only natural"
She said, "You gonna stay?" I said, "Yeah, I jes might"

Verse 13:
Isis, oh, Isis, you mystical child
What drives me to you is what drives me insane
I still can remember the way that you smiled
On the fifth day of May in the drizzlin' rain

Romance In Durango

Words & Music by Bob Dylan & Jacques Levy

Moderately

1. Hot chil - i pep-pers in the blist - er - ing sun____
(Verses 2-4 see block lyrics)

Dust on my face____ and my cape,____

Me and Mag - da - le - na on____ the run____

I think this time we shall es - cape.____

Sold my gui - tar to the bak - er's son____

For a few crumbs_ and a place to hide,___

But I can get an - oth - er one___ And I'll

play for Mag - da - le - na as we ride.___ *Chorus* No

llo - res, mi que - ri - da Di - os nos vi - gi - la____

Soon the horse___will take us to Du - ran - go. A -

-gar - ra - me, mi vi - da Soon the des - ert will be gone.__

Play 4 times Soon you will be danc - ing the fan - dan - go.

Verse 2:
Past the Aztec ruins and the ghosts of our people
Hoofbeats like castanets on stone
At night I dream of bells in the village steeple
Then I see the bloody face of Ramon
Was it me that shot him down in the cantina
Was it my hand that held the gun?
Come, let us fly, my Magdalena
The dogs are barking and what's done is done
Chorus:

Verse 3:
At the corrida we'll sit in the shade
And watch the young torero stand alone
We'll drink tequila where our grandfathers stayed
When they rode with Villa into Torreón
Then the padre will recite the prayers of old
In the little church this side of town
I will wear new boots and an earring of gold
You'll shine with diamonds in your wedding gown
The way is long but the end is near
Already the fiesta has begun
The face of God will appear
With His serpent eyes of obsidian
Chorus:

Verse 4:
Was that the thunder that I heard?
My head is vibrating, I feel a sharp pain
Come sit by me, don't say a word
Oh, can it be that I am slain?
Quick, Magdalena, take my gun
Look up in the hills, that flash of light
Aim well my little one
We may not make it through the night
Chorus:

Changing Of The Guards

Words & Music by Bob Dylan

Moderately

Capo fret 1

1. Six - teen years (six - teen years) six - teen___
(Verses 2-4 see block lyrics)

ban - ners u - ni - ted ov - er the field___

___ (ov - er the field) Where the good___ shep-herd grieves___

Des - per - ate men, (des - per - ate men) des - per - ate___

___ wo - men___ di - vi - ded Spread-ing their wings___ (spread - ing their

wings) 'neath___the fall - ing leaves.___ For - tune calls___

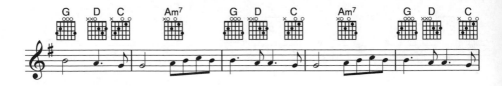

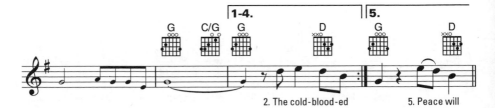

2. The cold-blood-ed   5. Peace will

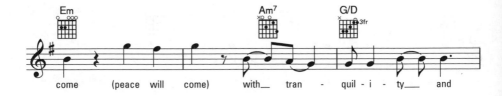

come (peace will come) with__ tran - quil - i - ty__ and

splen - dor on the wheels__ of fire____ (wheels of fire)____ But will bring__

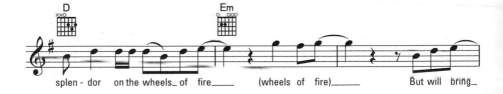

__ us no re - ward__ when her false i - dols fall (false i - dols

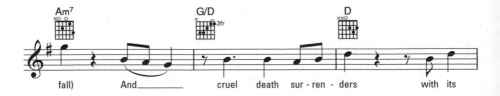

fall) And_____ cruel death sur - ren - ders with its

pale ghost re - treat - ing Be-tween the King and the Queen_ of swords.____

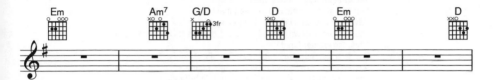

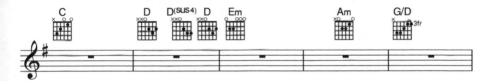

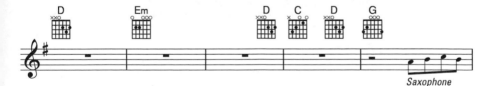

Saxophone

Repeat to fade

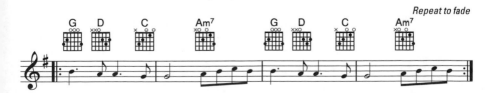

Verse 2:
The cold-blooded moon
The captain waits above the celebration
Sending his thoughts to a beloved maid
Whose ebony face is beyond communication
The captain is down but still believing that his love will be repaid
They shaved her head
She was torn between Jupiter and Apollo
A messenger arrived with a black nightingale
I seen her on the stairs and I couldn't help but follow
Follow her down as the fountain where they lifted her veil

Verse 3:
I stumbled to my feet
I rode past destruction in the ditches
With the stitches still mending 'neath a heart-shaped tattoo
Renegade priests and treacherous young witches
Were handing out the flowers that I'd given to you
The palace of mirrors
Where dog soldiers are reflected
The endless road and wailing of chimes
The empty rooms where her memory is protected
Where the angels' voices whisper to the souls of previous times

Verse 4:
She wakes him up
Forty-eight hours later, the sun is breaking
Near broken chains, mountain laurel and rolling rocks
She's begging to know what measures he now will be taking
He's pulling her down and she's clutching on to his long golden locks
Gentlemen, he said
I don't need your organization, I've shined your shoes
I've moved your mountains and marked your cards
But Eden is burning, either brace yourself for elimination
Or else your hearts must have the courage for the changing of the guards

Señor (Tales Of Yankee Power)

Words & Music by Bob Dylan

Slowly

1. Se - ñor, se -
(2.) - ñor, se -

- ñor, do you know where we're head - in'?_____ Lin - coln
- ñor, do you know where she is hid - in'?_____ How

Coun - ty Road_ or Ar - ma - ged - don?__ Seems like I been down this way be - fore._
long are we gon - na be rid - in'?___ How long must I keep my eyes glued to the door?_

___ Is there a - ny truth in that, se - ñor?_
___ Will there be an - y com - fort there, se - ñor?_

1.

2.

___ 2. Se - ___

There's a

213

wick-ed wind still blow - in' on that up-per deck, There's an
last thing I re - mem - ber be - fore I stripped and kneeled, Was that

i - ron cross still hang - ing down from a - round her neck. There's a
train-load of fools bogged down in a mag - net - ic field. A

march-in' band still play - in' in that va - cant lot Where she
gyp - sy with a bro - ken flag and a flash-ing ring Said,

held me in her arms one time and said, "For - get me not." 3. Se -
"Son, this ain't a dream no more, it's the real thing." 4. Se -

-ñor, se - ñor, I can
-ñor, se - ñor, you know their

see that paint - ed wag - on, I can smell the tail of the dra - gon.
hearts is as hard as lea - ther. Well, give me a min - ute, let me get it to - geth - er.

214

Can't stand the sus - pense an - y - more.
I just got - ta pick my - self up off the floor.
Can you

1.

Dm   Am

tell me who to con - tact here, se - ñor?   Well, the

Dm   Am

I'm rea - dy when you__ are, se - ñor.   5. Se -

Em   F   C

-ñor, se - ñor, let's dis - con - nect__ these ca - bles,

G/B Am   G

Ov - er - turn__ these ta - bles. This place don't make sense to me__ no

F   Dm   Am   **D.S.**
                                        (instrumental) and fade

more.   Can you tell me what we're wait-ing for, se-ñor?__

New Directions

Dylan saw out the 1970s with two albums—*Street Legal* and *Slow Train Coming*. The latter largely reflected his religious preoccupations of the time, and 'Gotta Serve Somebody' from that album gradually became a Dylan classic. In 1981 came *Shot Of Love*, featuring a return to secular songs with a few spiritual musings thrown in of which the sublime 'Every Grain Of Sand' was perhaps the standout example. *Infidels* produced 'Blind Willie McTell'...or at least would have done had it not been left off the album release: it later surfaced to considerable acclaim on one of the Dylan bootleg series. *Knocked Out Loaded* offered a bewildering mix of collaborations and cover songs including 'Brownsville Girl', a Dylan collaboration with Sam Shepard that clocked in at over eleven minutes. However, *Oh Mercy*, produced by Daniel Lanois and Dylan's 25th studio album, was generally hailed as a return to peak form. Recorded in New Orleans, performer/producer Lanois imposed his own stamp on the album and despite some creative tensions helped make it into a coherent whole that gave it more focus than *Infidels* or *Knocked Out Loaded*. This was to be the start of a renaissance in Dylan's career which coincided with an increased live schedule, dubbed by fans as the 'never-ending' tour. This intense commitment still sees him perform over 100 shows a year, drawing on songs from his entire catalogue.

Gotta Serve Somebody

Words & Music by Bob Dylan

Moderately slow

1. You may be an am-bas-sa-dor to Eng-land or France,___ You may like to gam-ble,

(Verses 2-7 see block lyrics)

you might like to dance,___ You may___ be the hea-vy-weight cham -

- pion of the world,___ You may be a so-cial-ite___ with a

Chorus

long___ string of pearls But you're gon-na have to serve some-bo-dy,

yes in-deed___ You're gon-na have to serve___ some-bo-dy. Well,

it may be the dev-il or___ it may be the Lord___ But you're gon-na have to

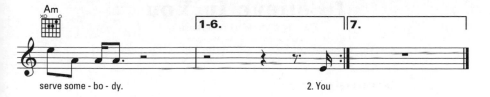

serve some - bo - dy.   2. You

Verse 2:
You might be a rock 'n' roll addict prancing on the stage
You might have drugs at your command, women in a cage
You may be a businessman or some high-degree thief
They may call you Doctor or they may call you Chief
Chorus:

Verse 3:
You may be a state trooper, you might be a young Turk
You may be the head of some big TV network
You may be rich or poor, you may be blind or lame
You may be living in another country under another name
Chorus:

Verse 4:
You may be a construction worker working on a home
You may be living in a mansion or you might live in a dome
You might own guns and you might even own tanks
You might be somebody's landlord, you might even own banks
Chorus:

Verse 5:
You may be a preacher with your spiritual pride
You may be a city councilman taking bribes on the side
You may be workin' in a barbershop, you may know how to cut hair
You may be somebody's mistress, may be somebody's heir
Chorus:

Verse 6:
Might like to wear cotton, might like to wear silk
Might like to drink whiskey, might like to drink milk
You might like to eat caviar, you might like to eat bread
You may be sleeping on the floor, sleeping in a king-sized bed
Chorus:

Verse 7:
You may call me Terry, you may call me Timmy
You may call me Bobby, you may call me Zimmy
You may call me R.J., you may call me Ray
You may call me anything but no matter what you say

(Chorus:)
You're gonna have to serve somebody, yes indeed
You're gonna have to serve somebody
Well, it may be the devil or it may be the Lord
But you're gonna have to serve somebody

I Believe In You

Words & Music by Bob Dylan

Moderately slowly

1. They ask me how I feel And if my love is real And how I know I'll

make it through. And they, they look at me and

frown, They'd like to drive me from this town, They don't want___ me a-

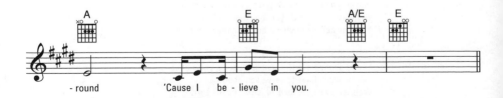

-round 'Cause I be - lieve in you.

2. They show me to the door, They say don't come back_ no more 'Cause I don't be like they'd like me to, And I walk out on my own A thou-sand miles_ from home But I don't feel a- -lone 'Cause I be-lieve in you. I be- -lieve in you ev-en through the tears_ and the laugh-ter, I be-

- lieve in you ev - en though we be a - part. I be -

- lieve in you ev - en on the morn - ing af - ter.

Oh, when the dawn is near - ing, Oh, when the night is dis - ap - pear - ing.

Oh, this feel - ing's still here in my heart.

3. Don't let me drift too far, Keep me where you

are Where I will al - ways be re - newed And

that which you've giv-en me___ to - day   Is worth more than I could

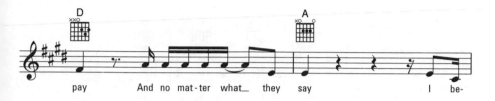

pay   And no mat-ter what___ they   say   I be-

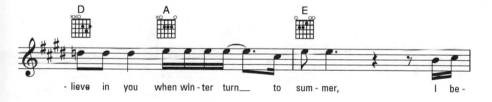

- lieve in   you.   I be -

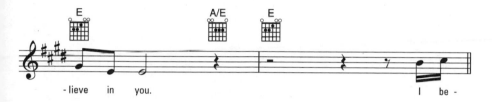

- lieve in   you when win-ter turn___ to sum - mer,   I be -

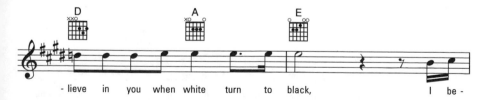

- lieve   in   you when white   turn   to   black,   I be -

- lieve   in   you ev-en though___ I   be   out - num-bered.

Oh, though the earth may shake me Oh, though my friends for - sake me

Oh, ev - en that couldn't make me go back.

4. Don't let me change my heart Keep me set a -

- part From all the plans they do pur - sue. And

I, I don't mind the pain Don't mind the driv - ing rain I know I will sus -

-tain 'Cause I be - lieve in you.

Every Grain Of Sand

Words & Music by Bob Dylan

Moderately slow, in 2

Capo fret 8

1. In the
time of my con - fes - sion, in the hour of my deep - est need

(Verse 2 see block lyrics)

When the pool of tears be - neath my feet flood ev - 'ry new - born

seed There's a dy - in' voice with - in me reach - ing out some

- where, Toil - ing in the dan - ger and in the mor - als___ of___ des -

- pair. Don't have the in - cli - na - tion to look back on an - y mis -

225

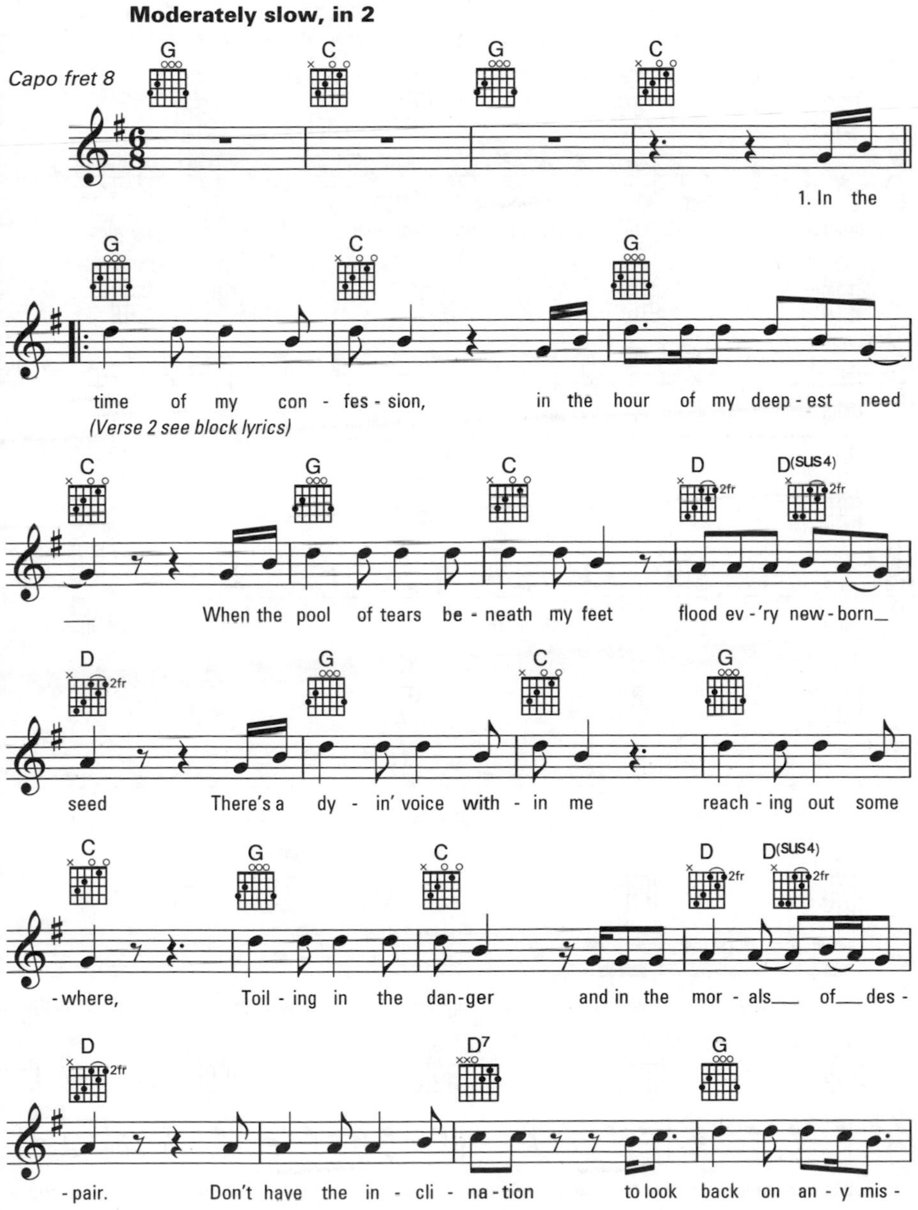

-take, Like Cain, I now be-hold this chain of e-vents that I____ must

break. In the fu-ry____ of the mo-ment I can see the Mas-ter's

hand In ev-'ry leaf that trem-bles, in ev-'ry grain____ of

1. sand. **2.** 2. Oh, the sand. 3. I have

gone from rags to rich-es in the sor-row of the night In the

vi-o lence____ of a sum-mer's dream, in the chill of a win-try light, In the

bit-ter dance of lone-li-ness fad-ing____ in-to space In the

226

bro - ken mir - ror of in - no-cence on each for - got- ten___ face. I

hear the an - cient foot-steps like the mo - tion of___ the sea Some-

- times I turn, there's some-one there, oth-er times it's on - ly me. I am

hang - ing in the bal-ance___ of the re - al - i - ty of man Like

ev - 'ry___ spar-row fall - ing, like ev - 'ry grain___ of sand.

Verse 2:
Oh, the flowers of indulgence and the weeds of yesteryear
Like criminals, they have choked the breath of conscience and good cheer
The sun beat down upon the steps of time to light the way
To ease the pain of idleness and the memory of decay
I gaze into the doorway of temptation's angry flame
And every time I pass that way I always hear my name
Then onward in my journey I come to understand
That every hair is numbered like every grain of sand

Jokerman

Words & Music by Bob Dylan

Brightly

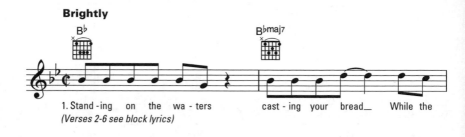

1. Stand-ing on the wa-ters cast-ing your bread__ While the
(Verses 2-6 see block lyrics)

eyes of the i-dol with the i-ron head___ are glow - ing.

Dis - tant ships sail-ing in - to the mist,__ You were

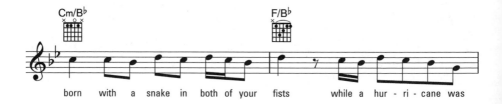

born with a snake in both of your fists while a hur - ri - cane was

blow - ing.___ Free-dom just

228

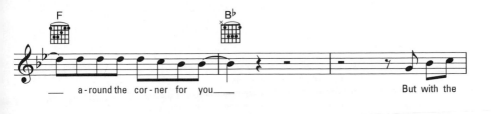

a - round the cor - ner for you___ But with the

truth so far off, what good will it do?___

Chorus

Jok - er - man dance to the night - in - gale tune, Bird___

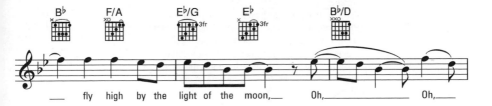

___ fly high by the light of the moon,___ Oh,___ Oh,___

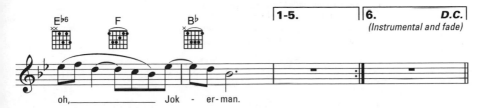

1-5. | **6.** *D.C.*
(Instrumental and fade)

oh,___ Jok - er - man.

Verse 2:
So swiftly the sun sets in the sky
You rise up and say goodbye to no one
Fools rush in where angels fear to tread
Both of their futures, so full of dread, you don't show one
Shedding off one more layer of skin
Keeping one step ahead of the persecutor within
Chorus:

Verse 3:
You're a man of the mountains, you can walk on the clouds
Manipulator of crowds, you're a dream twister
You're going to Sodom and Gomorrah
But what do you care? Ain't nobody there would want to marry your sister
Friend to the martyr, a friend to the woman of shame
You look into the fiery furnace, see the rich man without any name
Chorus:

Verse 4:
Well, the Book of Leviticus and Deuteronomy
The law of the jungle and the sea are your only teachers
In the smoke of the twilight on a milk-white steed
Michelangelo indeed could've carved out your features
Resting in the fields, far from the turbulent space
Half asleep near the stars with a small dog licking your face
Chorus:

Verse 5:
Well, the rifleman's stalking the sick and the lame
Preacherman seeks the same, who'll get there first is uncertain
Nightsticks and water cannons, tear gas, padlocks
Molotov cocktails and rocks behind every curtain
False-hearted judges dying in the webs that they spin
Only a matter of time 'til night comes steppin' in
Chorus:

Verse 6:
It's a shadowy world, skies are slippery gray
A woman just gave birth to a prince today and dressed him in scarlet
He'll put the priest in his pocket, put the blade to the heat
Take the motherless children off the street
And place them at the feet of a harlot
Oh, Jokerman, you know what he wants
Oh, Jokerman, you don't show any response
Chorus:

Blind Willie McTell

Words & Music by Bob Dylan

To match original recording, tune down one semitone

231

And I____ know no____ one can____ sing the blues Like

Blind Wil-lie_____ Mc - Tell._____   2. Well, I

3. See them big__plan-ta-tions burn-ing,   Hear the crack-ing of__ the whips_
(Verse 4 see block lyrics)

Smell that sweet mag-no - lia bloom-ing,__   See the ghosts_

__ of_____ slav-er - y ships._____   I can

hear them tribes_ a - moan-ing,_____   (I can) hear that un-der-tak - er's

bell;   No - bo-dy____ can sing the blues_____

232

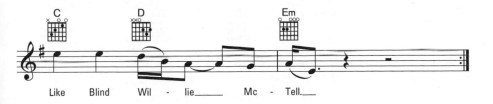

Like Blind Wil - lie_____ Mc - Tell._____

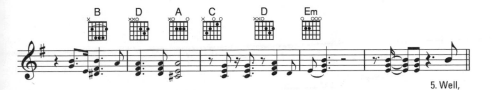

5. Well,

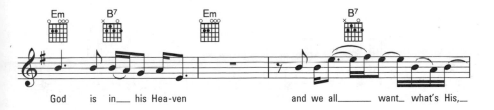

God is in___ his Hea - ven and we all_____ want_ what's His,__

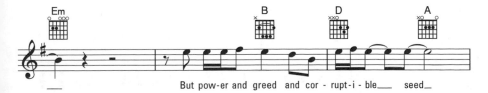

___ But pow-er and greed and cor - rupt-i - ble___ seed__

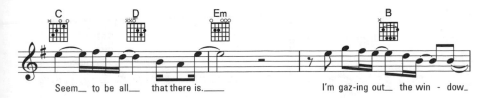

Seem_ to be all___ that there is._____ I'm gaz-ing out_ the win - dow_

233

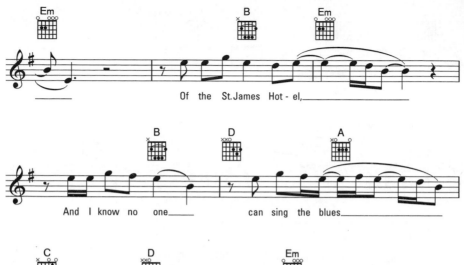

Of the St. James Hot - el, _____

And I know no one _____ can sing the blues _____

Like Blind Wil - lie _____ Mc - Tell. _____

Instrumental

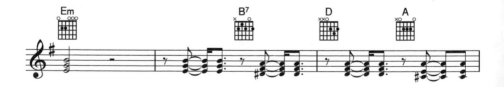

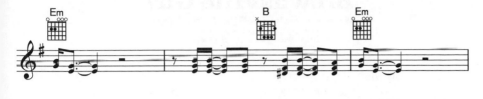

rit.

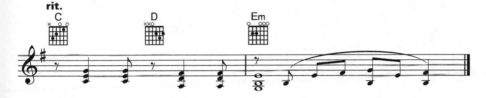

Verse 2:
Well, I heard that hoot owl singing
As they were taking down the tents
The stars above the barren trees
Was his only audience
Them charcoal gypsy maidens
Can strut their feathers well
But nobody can sing the blues
Like Blind Willie McTell

Verse 4:
There's a woman by the river
With some fine young handsome man
He's dressed up like a squire
Bootlegged whiskey in his hand
There's a chain gang on the highway
I can hear them rebels yell
And I know no one can sing the blues
Like Blind Willie McTell

Brownsville Girl

Words & Music by Bob Dylan & Sam Sheppard

Slowly

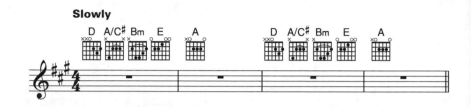

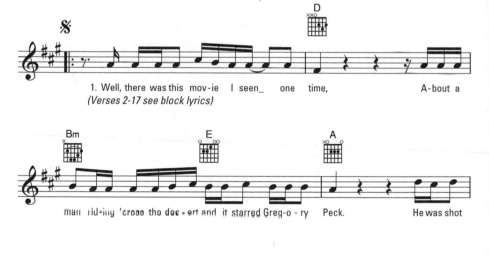

1. Well, there was this mov-ie I seen_ one time, A-bout a
(Verses 2-17 see block lyrics)

man rid-ing 'cross the des-ert and it starred Greg-o-ry Peck. He was shot

down by a hun-gry kid_ try'n' to make a name for him-self. The towns-peo-ple want-ed to

1-5, 7-9, 11-13, 15-16.

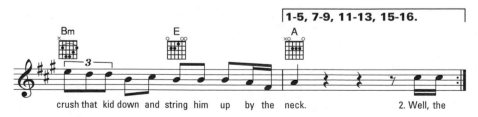

crush that kid down and string him up by the neck. 2. Well, the

6, 10, 14, 17.

Chorus

- trol.   Browns-ville girl   with your Browns-ville curls,_

teeth   like   pearls___shin-ing   like   the moon   a - bove.___

Browns - ville   girl,   show   me   all   a - round   the   world,_

Verses 7, 11 & 15 **D.S.**
Last time Chorus to fade

Browns - ville   girl,   you're   my   hon - ey   love.

Verse 2:
Well, the marshal, now he beat that kid to a bloody pulp
As the dying gunfighter lay in the sun and gasped for his last breath
"Turn him loose, let him go, let him say he outdrew me fair and square
I want him to feel what it's like to every moment face his death"

Verse 3:
Well, I keep seeing this stuff and it just comes a-rolling in
And you know it blows right through me like a ball and chain
You know I can't believe we've lived so long and are still so far apart
The memory of you keeps callin' after me like a rollin' train

Verse 4:
I can still see the day that you came to me on the painted desert
In your busted down Ford and your platform heels
I could never figure out why you chose that particular place to meet
Ah, but you were right. It was perfect as I got in behind the wheel

Verse 5:
Well, we drove that car all night into San Anton'
And we slept near the Alamo, your skin was so tender and soft
Way down in Mexico you went out to find a doctor and you never came back
I would have gone on after you but I didn't feel like letting my head get blown off

Verse 6:
Well, we're drivin' this car and the sun is comin' up over the Rockies
Now I know she ain't you but she's here and she's got that dark rhythm in her soul
But I'm too over the edge and I ain't in the mood anymore to remember the times when I was your only man
And she don't want to remind me. She knows this car would go out of control
Chorus:

Verse 7:
Well, we crossed the panhandle and then we headed towards Amarillo
We pulled up where Henry Porter used to live. He owned a wreckin' lot outside of town about a mile
Ruby was in the backyard hanging clothes, she had her red hair tied back. She saw us come rolling up in a trail of dus
She said, "Henry ain't here but you can come on in, he'll be back in a little while"

Verse 8:
Then she told us how times were tough and about how she was thinkin' of bummin' a ride back to where she started
But ya know, she changed the subject every time money came up
She said, "Welcome to the land of the living dead" You could tell she was so broken hearted
She said, "Even the swap meets around here are getting pretty corrupt"

Verse 9:
"How far are y'all going?" Ruby asked us with a sigh
"We're going all the way 'til the wheels fall off and burn
'Til the sun peels the paint and the seat covers fade and the water moccasin dies"
Ruby just smiled and said, "Ah, you know some babies never learn"

Verse 10:
Something about that movie though, well I just can't get it out of my head
But I can't remember why I was in it or what part I was supposed to play
All I remember about it was Gregory Peck and the way people moved
And a lot of them seemed to be lookin' my way
Chorus:

Verse 11:
Well, they were looking for somebody with a pompadour
I was crossin' the street when shots rang out
I didn't know whether to duck or to run, so I ran
"We got him cornered in the churchyard," I heard somebody shout

Verse 12:
Well, you saw my picture in the *Corpus Christi Tribune*. Underneath it, it said, "A man with no alibi"
You went out on a limb to testify for me, you said I was with you
Then when I saw you break down in front of the judge and cry real tears
It was the best acting I saw anybody do

Verse 13:
Now I've always been the kind of person that doesn't like to trespass but sometimes you just find yourself over the line
Oh if there's an original thought out there, I could use it right now
You know, I feel pretty good, but that ain't sayin' much. I could feel a whole lot better
If you were just here by my side to show me how

Verse 14:
Well, I'm standin' in line in the rain to see a movie starring Gregory Peck
Yeah, but you know it's not the one that I had in mind
He's got a new one out now, I don't even know what it's about
But I'll see him in anything so I'll stand in line
Chorus:

Verse 15:
You know, it's funny how things never turn out the way you had 'em planned
The only thing we knew for sure about Henry Porter is that his name wasn't Henry Porter
And you know there was somethin' about you baby that I liked that was always too good for this world
Just like you always said there was somethin' about me you liked that I left behind in the French Quarter

Verse 16:
Strange how people who suffer together have stronger connections than people who are most content
I don't have any regrets, they can talk about me plenty when I'm gone
You always said people don't do what they believe in, they just do what's most convenient, then they repent
And I always said, "Hang on to me, baby, and let's hope that the roof stays on"

Verse 17:
There was a movie I seen one time, I think I sat through it twice
I don't remember who I was or where I was bound
All I remember about it was it starred Gregory Peck, he wore a gun and he was shot in the back
Seems like a long time ago, long before the stars were torn down
Chorus:

Most Of The Time

Words & Music by Bob Dylan

I would-n't change it if I could, I can make it all match up,

I can hold my own, I can deal_ with the si - tu - a - tion

right down to the bone, I can sur-vive,___ I can en-dure___ And I don't e-ven

think a-bout her Most of the time.___

3. Most of the time___ My head is on straight,_ Most of the time_

I'm strong e-nough not to hate. I don't build up il - lu - sion

'til it makes me sick,_ I ain't a-fraid of con - fu - sion

no mat-ter how thick. I can smile in the face__ of man-

kind. Don't e-ven re - mem-ber what her lips_ felt like on mine Most of the

time.__ Most of the time_

She ain't e - ven in my mind, I would-n't know her if I saw her,

She's that far be - hind. Most of the time__

I can't e - ven be sure_ If she was ev - er with me__

Or if I was ev - er with her.___ 4. Most of the time

242

I'm half_ way con-tent,_ Most of the time_ I know ex-act-ly where it went, I don't cheat on my-self,_ I don't run and hide,_ Hide from the feel-ings that are bur-ied in-side._ I don't com-pro-mise_ and I don't pre-tend,_ I don't e-ven care if I ev-er see her a-gain_ Most_ of the time._

Repeat to fade

Ring Them Bells

Words & Music by Bob Dylan

Moderately slow

Capo fret 1

1. Ring them bells, ye hea-then From the ci - ty that dreams,____

(Verse 2 see block lyrics)

Ring them bells from the sanc - tu - ar-ies 'Cross the val-leys and streams,____ For they're

deep and they're wide____ And the world's on its side____ And

1.

time is run - ning back - wards And____ so is the bride.

245

man -y_____ when the game is through. Ring them bells, for the time that

flies, For the child that cries When in-no-cence dies.

4. Ring them bells Saint Cath-'rine From the top of the room, Ring them from the

for - tress For the lil - ies that bloom._____ Oh the lines are long,

_____ And the fight - ing is strong And they're break-ing down the

dis -tance Be-tween right and wrong._____

Verse 2:
Ring them bells St. Peter
Where the four winds blow
Ring them bells with an iron hand
So the people will know
Oh it's rush hour now
On the wheel and the plow
And the sun is going down
Upon the sacred cow

Everything Is Broken

Words & Music by Bob Dylan

1. Bro-ken lines, bro-ken strings, bro-ken threads, bro-ken springs._ Bro-ken i-dols, bro-ken heads, peo-ple sleep-ing in bro-ken beds. Ain't no use jiv-ing, ain't no use jok-ing, ev--'ry-thing is bro-ken.

2. Bro-ken bot-tles, bro-ken plates,_ bro-ken switch-es, bro-ken gates._ Bro-ken dish-es, bro-ken parts, streets are filled_ with bro-ken hearts.

Bro-ken words ne-ver meant to be spo-ken, ev - 'ry-thing is bro-ken.

Seems like ev-'ry-time you stop and turn a-round,

some-thing else_ just hit the ground._ 3. Bro-ken cut-ters, bro-ken saws,_

bro-ken buc-kles, bro-ken laws. Bro-ken bo-dies, bro-ken bones,

bro-ken voi-ces on bro-ken phones. Take a deep breath,_

feel like you're cho-kin', ev - 'ry-thing is bro-ken.

248

Ev-'ry-time you leave and go off some-place, things fall to pie-ces in my face.

4. Bro-ken hands_ on bro-ken ploughs, bro-ken trea-ties,

bro-ken vows._ Bro-ken pipes,_ bro-ken tools,_

peo-ple bend-ing bro-ken rules.___ Hound dog howl-ing,

bull-frog croak-ing, ev - 'ry-thing is bro-ken.

Man In The Long Black Coat

Words & Music by Bob Dylan

2. Some - bo-dy seen him hang-ing a-round At the old dance hall on the out - skirts of town. He looked in - to her eyes when she stopped him to ask If he want-ed to dance, he had a face like a mask. Some - bo - dy said_ from the Bi - ble he'd quote There was dust on the man In the long black coat.

3. Preach-er was a-talk- in', there's a ser-mon he gave, He said ev-'ry man's con-science is

vile and de- praved, You can- not de- pend on it to be your guide When it's

you who must keep it sa - tis - fied.

It ain't ea-sy to swal-low it sticks in the throat, She gave her

heart to the man In the long black coat. There

are no___ mis-takes in life some peo - ple say It is true some- times you can

see it that way. But peo-ple don't live or die, peo-ple just float. She

went   with the man   In the   long   black   coat.   4. There's

smoke   on the wa-ter,   it's   been there since June,   Tree trunks up-root-ed 'neath the

high   cres-cent moon   Feel the pulse   and vi - bra-tion   and the rumb-ling   force

Some-bo - dy   is   out there   beat-ing   a dead   horse.

She nev - er   said no-thing,   there was   no-thing   she wrote,   She

gone   with the man   In the   long   black   coat.

253

Dignity

Words & Music by Bob Dylan

To match original recording, tune down one semitone

Moderately

1. Fat man look-in' in a___ blade of steel___
(Verses 2-4 see block lyrics)

Thin man look-in' at his last meal

Hol-low man look-in' in a cot-ton-field___ For

dig-ni-ty___ Wise man look-in' in a

blade of grass Young man look-in' in the

sha-dows that pass___ Poor man look-in' through paint-ed

glass   For dig - ni - ty

Some - bo - dy got mur-dered on___ New Year's Eve

Some - bo - dy said dig - ni - ty was the first to leave

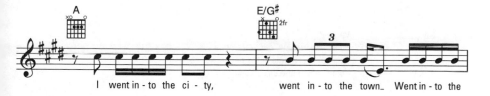

I went in - to the ci - ty,   went in - to the town_ Went in - to the

land of the mid - night sun

Search-in' high,_   search-in' low_   Search-in' ev - 'ry - where_

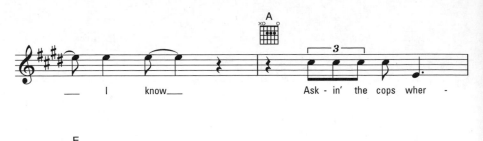

— I know___ Ask - in' the cops wher -

- ev - er I go Have you seen

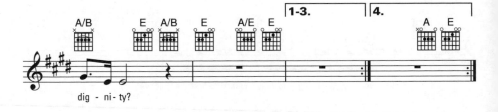

dig - ni - ty?

Verse 2:
Blind man breakin' out of a trance
Puts both his hands in the pockets of chance
Hopin' to find one circumstance
Of dignity

I went to the wedding of Mary Lou
She said "I don't want nobody see me talkin' to you"
Said she could get killed if she told me what she knew
About dignity

I went down where the vultures feed
I would've got deeper, but there wasn't any need
Heard the tongues of angels and the tongues of men
Wasn't any difference to me

Chilly wind sharp as a razor blade
House on fire, debts unpaid
Gonna stand at the window, gonna ask the maid
Have you seen dignity?

Verse 3:
Drinkin' man listens to the voice he hears
In a crowded room full of covered-up mirrors
Lookin' into the lost forgotten years
For dignity

Met Prince Phillip at the home of the blues
Said he'd give me information if his name wasn't used
He wanted money up front, said he was abused
By dignity

Footprints runnin' cross the silver sand
Steps goin' down into tattoo land
I met the sons of darkness and the sons of light
In the bordertowns of despair

Got no place to fade, got no coat
I'm on the rollin' river in a jerkin' boat
Tryin' to read a note somebody wrote
About dignity

Verse 4:
Sick man lookin' for the doctor's cure
Lookin' at his hands for the lines that were
And into every masterpiece of literature
For dignity

Englishman stranded in the blackheart wind
Combin' his hair back, his future looks thin
Bites the bullet and he looks within
For dignity

Someone showed me a picture and I just laughed
Dignity never been photographed
I went into the red, went into the black
Into the valley of dry bone dreams

So many roads, so much at stake
So many dead ends, I'm at the edge of the lake
Sometimes I wonder what it's gonna take
To find dignity

Series Of Dreams

Words & Music by Bob Dylan

Not too fast

1. I was

think-ing___ of a se-ries of___ dreams Where
(Verse 2 see block lyrics)

no thing comes up to the top Ev-'ry

-thing stays down where it's wound-ed And

comes to a per-ma-nent stop Was-n't

259

seemed   to be do-ing was   climb   Was-n't

look-ing   for a - ny spe-cial as - sist-ance,   Not

go-ing   to a - ny great ex - tremes_   I'd al-

- rea -dy   gone the dis-tance   Just

think-ing   of a se - ries of   dreams.

Verse 2:
Thinking of a series of dreams
Where the time and the tempo fly
And there's no exit in any direction
'Cept the one that you can't see with your eyes
Wasn't making any great connection
Wasn't falling for any intricate scheme
Nothing that would pass inspection
Just thinking of a series of dreams

Back On Track

Remarkably, the last two decades of Dylan's career have seen some of his most acclaimed and successful work in a series of superb new albums. A further collaboration with Lanois in 1997 produced *Time Out Of Mind*, featuring the songs 'Not Dark Yet' and 'Make You Feel My Love', modern Dylan songs which stand up against his best work of the 60s and 70s. If anything, *Love and Theft* (2001) was even further fêted, with the song 'Mississippi' (held over from the previous album) a standout. Then came two more studio albums bringing new success: *Modern Times* in 2006 — which entered the *Billboard* charts at No. 1 — and the best-selling *Together Through Life* in 2009. As well as these highlights, Dylan was to receive an Oscar for 'Things Have Changed' from *The Wonder Boys* in 2000 and was the inspiration for two high-profile movie biographies in Martin Scorsese's epic documentary *No Direction Home* and Todd Hayne's *I'm Not There* which featured a selection of Hollywood A-listers playing the lead role. Further recognition came in 2008 with the award to Bob Dylan of a special Pulitzer Prize (the first ever given to a rock musician) for "lyrical compositions of extraordinary poetic power" that have had a "profound impact on popular music and American culture". Whatever is next for Dylan (ever-unpredictable, his next record was to be a charity Christmas record of holiday standards), there is no doubting the significance of his extraordinary artistic legacy.

Love Sick

Words & Music by Bob Dylan

264

Verse 3:
I see, I see lovers in the meadow
I see, I see silhouettes in the window
I watch them 'til they're gone and they leave me hanging on
To a shadow
I'm sick of love; I hear the clock tick
This kind of love; I'm love sick

Verse 4:
Instrumental

Verse 5:
Sometimes the silence can be like the thunder
Sometimes I wanna take to the road and plunder
Could you ever be true?
I think of you
And I wonder
I'm sick of love; I wish I'd never met you
I'm sick of love; I'm trying to forget you
Just don't know what to do
I'd give anything to be with you

Tryin' To Get To Heaven

Words & Music by Bob Dylan

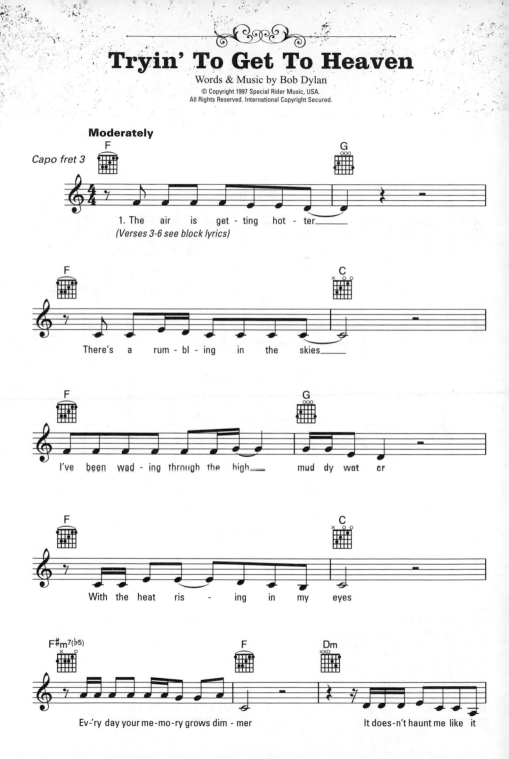

Moderately

Capo fret 3

1. The air is get-ting hot-ter
(Verses 3-6 see block lyrics)

There's a rum-bl-ing in the skies

I've been wad-ing through the high mud-dy wat-er

With the heat ris-ing in my eyes

Ev-'ry day your me-mo-ry grows dim-mer

It does-n't haunt me like it

did be - fore___ I've been walk - ing through the mid -

- dle of no - where_ Trying to get_ to heav'n_ be- fore_ they close

___ the door 2. When I was in Mis - sou - ri

They would not let___ me be I had to leave there in a

hur - ry I on - ly saw what they let___ me see

You broke a heart that loved___ you___ Now you can

267

seal up the book   and not   write an-y-more   I've been walk-ing that lone-some

val - ley   Try'n to get___ to heav'n__ be-fore_ they close

1-3.   **4.**

___ the door

Verse 3:
People on the platforms
Waiting for the trains
I can hear their hearts a-beatin'
Like pendulums swinging on chains
I tried to give you everything
That your heart was longing for
I'm just going down the road feeling bad
Trying to get to heaven before they close the door

Verse 4:
Instrumental

Verse 5:
I'm going down the river
Down to New Orleans
They tell me everything is gonna be all right
But I don't know what "all right" even means
I was riding in a buggy with Miss Mary-Jane
Miss Mary-Jane got a house in Baltimore
I been all around the world, boys
Now I'm trying to get to heaven before they close the door

Verse 6:
Gonna sleep down in the parlor
And relive my dreams
I'll close my eyes and I wonder
If everything is as hollow as it seems
Some trains don't pull no gamblers
No midnight ramblers, like they did before
I been to Sugar Town, I shook the sugar down
Now I'm trying to get to heaven before they close the door

Make You Feel My Love

Words & Music by Bob Dylan

Moderately slow

Capo fret 1

1. When the rain___ is blow - ing in your face

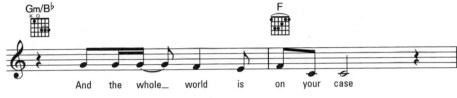

And the whole___ world is on your case

I could of - fer you a warm em - brace

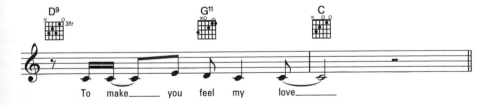

To make_____ you feel my love_____

2. When the eve - ning sha - dows and the stars ap - pear

(Verse 4 see block lyrics)

And there is no one there to dry___ your tears___

I could hold you for a mil - lion years

To make you feel my love___

I know you have - n't made your mind up yet___
(Vocal 2º)

But I would nev - er do___ you wrong

I've known it from the mo - ment that we met___

No doubt in my mind where you be - long_____

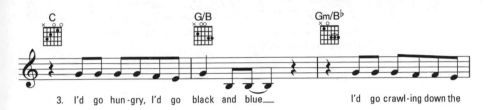

3. I'd go hun-gry, I'd go black and blue___ I'd go crawl-ing down the

av - en - ue_____ There is no - thing that I

would-n't do To make you feel my love

Verse 4:
(8 bars instrumental)
The storms are raging on the rollin' sea
And on the highway of regret
The winds of change are blowing wild and free
You ain't seen nothing like me yet
I could make you happy, make your dreams come true
Nothing that I wouldn't do
Go to the ends of the earth for you
To make you feel my love

Not Dark Yet

Words & Music by Bob Dylan

Moderately slow

1. Sha-dows are fall-ing
(Verses 2-5 see block lyrics)
and I've been here all day

It's too hot to sleep, time is run-ning a - way

Feel like my soul has_ turned_ in-to steel_

I've still got the scars_ that the sun did-n't heal_

There's not e-ven room e-nough to be_ an-y -where

272

It's not dark yet,___ but it's___ get-ting there.

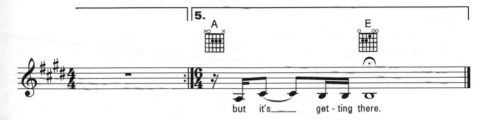

but it's___ get - ting there.

Verse 2:
Well, my sense of humanity has gone down the drain
Behind every beautiful thing there's been some kind of pain
She wrote me a letter and she wrote it so kind
She put down in writing what was in her mind
I just don't see why I should even care
It's not dark yet, but it's getting there

Verse 3:
Well, I've been to London and I've been to gay Paree
I've followed the river and I got to the sea
I've been down on the bottom of a world full of lies
I ain't looking for nothing in anyone's eyes
Sometimes my burden seems more than I can bear
It's not dark yet, but it's getting there

Verse 4:
Instrumental

Verse 5:
I was born here and I'll die here against my will
I know it looks like I'm moving, but I'm standing still
Every nerve in my body is so vacant and numb
I can't even remember what it was I came here to get away from
Don't even hear a murmur of a prayer
It's not dark yet, but it's getting there

273

Mississippi

Words & Music by Bob Dylan

Moderately

Guitar

1. Ev-'ry step of the way___ we walk the line,___
(Verses 4 & 7 see block lyrics)

your days are num - bered, so are mine.___

Time is pil - in' up,___ we strug-gle and we scrape,

we're all___ boxed in,___ no-where to es - cape.___

2. Cit - y's just a jun-gle, more games to play,___
(Verses 5 & 8 see block lyrics)

trapped in the heart of it, try'n to get a - way.___ I was

raised in the coun - try, I been work-in' in the town,__

I been in trou-ble ev - er since I set my suit-case down.

Bridge 1

1.Got no-thin' for you, I had no-thin' be-fore,___
(Bridges 2 & 3 see block lyrics)

don't ev - en have a - ny-thing for my - self___ a - ny-more.

Sky full of fire,___ pain pour-in' down,___

275

no-thin' you can sell___ me, I'll see you a - round.___

3. All my pow-ers of ex - pres-sion and thoughts so sub - lime___
(Verses 6 & 9 see block lyrics)

could nev-er do you jus - tice in rea - son or rhyme.___

On - ly one___ thing___ I did wrong,___

Play 3 times

stayed in Mis-sis - sip-pi a day___ too___ long.___

rit.

Guitar

276

Verse 4:
Well, the devil's in the alley, mule's in the stall
Say anything you wanna, I have heard it all
I was thinkin' 'bout the things that Rosie said
I was dreamin' I was sleepin' in Rosie's bed

Verse 5:
Walkin' through the leaves fallin' from the trees
Feelin' like a stranger nobody sees
So many things that we never will undo
I know you're sorry, I'm sorry too

Bridge 2:
Some people will offer you their hand and some won't
Last night I knew ya, tonight I don't
I need somethin' strong to distract my mind
I'm gonna look at you 'til my eyes go blind

Verse 6:
Well I got here followin' the southern star
I crossed that river just to be where you are
Only one thing I did wrong
Stayed in Mississippi a day too long

Verse 7:
Well my ship's been split to splinters and it's sinkin' fast
I'm drownin' in the poison, got no future, got no past
But my heart is not weary, it's light and it's free
I got nothin' but affection for all those who've sailed with me

Verse 8:
Everybody movin' if they ain't already there
Everybody got to move somewhere
Stick with me baby, stick with me anyhow
Things should start to get interestin' right about now

Bridge 3:
My clothes are wet, tight on my skin
Not as tight as the corner that I painted myself in
I know that fortune is waitin' to be kind
So give me your hand and say you'll be mine

Verse 9:
Well, the emptiness is endless, cold as the clay
You can always come back, but you can't come back all the way
Only one thing I did wrong
Stayed in Mississippi a day too long

High Water (For Charley Patton)

Words & Music by Bob Dylan

With a country bounce

1. High wa-ter ris - in', ris - in' night and day,

All the gold___ and sil - ver are be - in' stol - en a - way.___ Big Joe

Turn - er look - in' east___ and west From the dark-room of his mind, He

made to Kan - sas Ci - ty, Twelfth___ Street and Vine

No - thin' stand - ing there,_____

High wa - ter ev - 'ry - where.___

2. High wa - ter ris - in', the shacks are slid - in' down,__
(Verses 3-7 see block lyrics)

Folks lose their pos - ses - sions folks__ are leav - in' town.__ Ber - tha

Ma - son shook it— broke it, then she hung it on a wall,__ says, "You're

danc - in' with whom they tell you to,__ Or you don't dance at all"_____ It's

F5   F#5   G5   F5   G5   F5

tough out there,_____

G5   F5   F#5   G5 | 1-5. | | 6. |

High wa - ter ev - 'ry - where. 3. I got a

Instrumental fade to end

279

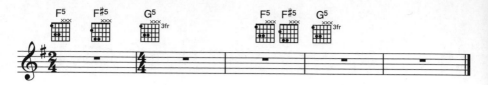

Verse 3:
I got a cravin' love for blazing speed
Got a hopped-up Mustang Ford
Jump into the wagon, love, throw your panties on the board
I can write you poems, make a strong man lose his mind
I'm no pig without a wig
I hope you treat me kind
Things are breakin' up out there
High water everywhere

Verse 4:
High water risin' six inches 'bove my head
Coffins droppin' in the street
Like balloons made out of lead
Water pourin' into Vicksburg, don't know what I'm gonna do
"Don't reach out for me," she said
"Can't you see I'm drownin' too?"
It's rough out there
High water everywhere

Verse 5:
Well, George Lewis told the Englishman, the Italian and the Jew
"You can't open up your mind, boys
To every conceivable point of view"
They got Charles Darwin trapped out there on Highway Five
Judge says to the High Sheriff
"I want him dead or alive
Either one, I don't care"
High water everywhere

Verse 6:
The Cuckoo is a pretty bird, she warbles as she flies
I'm preachin' the Word of God
I'm puttin' out your eyes
I asked Fat Nancy for somethin' to eat, she said, "Take it off the shelf –
As great as you are a man
You'll never be greater than yourself"
I told her I didn't really care
High water everywhere

Verse 7:
I'm gettin' up in the morning – I believe I'll dust my broom
Keeping away from the women
I'm givin' 'em lots of room
Thunder rolling over Clarksdale, everything is looking blue
I just can't be happy, love
Unless you're happy too
It's bad out there
High water everywhere

Things Have Changed

Words & Music by Bob Dylan

Moderately fast

Capo fret 3

1. A wor-ried man with a wor-ried mind No one in front of me and

(Verses 2-4 see block lyrics)

no-thing be - hind__ There's a wo-man on my lap__ and she's drink-ing cham -

- pagne__ Got white skin, got as - sas-sin's eyes_

I'm look-ing up in - to the sap - phire -tint - ed skies_ I'm well__ dressed,

wait-ing on the last train_

Bridge

Stand-ing on the gal-lows with my_

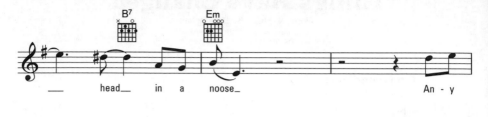

_____ head_____ in a noose_____   An - y

min - ute now I'm ex - pect-ing all   hell_____ to break   loose

Chorus

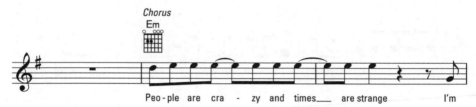

Peo - ple are cra - zy and times____ are strange   I'm

locked in   tight,____   I'm   out of range   I   used to care,   but

things have changed._____

Play 4 times

282

Verse 2:
This place ain't doing me any good
I'm in the wrong town, I should be in Hollywood
Just for a second there I thought I saw something move
Gonna take dancing lessons do the jitterbug rag
Ain't no shortcuts, gonna dress in drag
Only a fool in here would think he's got anything to prove

Bridge 2:
Lot of water under the bridge, lot of other stuff too
Don't get up gentlemen, I'm only passing through
Chorus:

Verse 3:
I've been walking forty miles of bad road
If the Bible is right, the world will explode
I've been trying to get as far away from myself as I can
Some things are too hot to touch
The human mind can only stand so much
You can't win with a losing hand

Bridge 3:
Feel like falling in love with the first woman I meet
Putting her in a wheelbarrow and wheeling her down the street
Chorus:

Verse 4:
I hurt easy, I just don't show it
You can hurt someone and not even know it
The next sixty seconds could be like an eternity
Gonna get low down, gonna fly high
All the truth in the world adds up to one big lie
I'm in love with a woman who don't even appeal to me

Bridge 4:
Mr. Jinx and Miss Lucy, they jumped in the lake
I'm not that eager to make a mistake
Chorus:

Workingman's Blues #2

Words & Music by Bob Dylan

1. There's an eve - nin' haze set - tlin' ov - er the town

(Verses 3, 5 & 7 see block lyrics)

star - light by the edge of the creek___ The buy in' power of the pro - le - tar-iat's gone down mon - ey's get-tin' shal-low and weak___ The place I love best is a sweet me - mo - ry___ It's a

new   path   that   we   trod_____   They   say

low   wa - ges   are   re - al - i - ty   If   we

want   to   com - pete   a - broad_____

2. My   cruel   wea - pons   have   been   put   on   the   shelf_____   come
(Verses 4, 6 & 8 see block lyrics)

___   sit   down___   on   my   knee_____   You   are

dear - er   to   me   than   my - self   As

you   your - self   can   see_____   I'm

285

lis - ten - in' to the steel rails_____ hum

Got both eyes_____ tight shut Just

sit - ting here trying to keep the hun - ger from

Creep - ing it's way_____ in - to my gut

Chorus

Meet me at the bot - tom, don't lag be - hind_____

Bring me my boots and shoes_____ You can

hang back or fight your best on_____ the front line

Sing a lit - tle___ bit___ of these work - ing - man's blues.___

1, 2, 3.　　**4.**

3. Now, I'm

Begin fading, instrumental

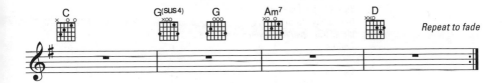

Repeat to fade

Verse 3:
Now, I'm sailin' on back, ready for the long haul
Tossed by the winds and the seas
I'll drag 'em all down to hell and I'll stand 'em at the wall
I'll sell 'em to their enemies
I'm tryin' to feed my soul with thought
Gonna sleep off the rest of the day
Sometimes no one wants what we got
Sometimes you can't give it away

Now the place is ringed with countless foes
Some of them may be deaf and dumb
No man, no woman knows
The hour that sorrow will come
In the dark I hear the night birds call
I can hear a lover's breath
I sleep in the kitchen with my feet in the hall
Sleep is like a temporary death
Chorus:

Verse 5:
Well, they burned my barn, they stole my horse
I can't save a dime
I got to be careful, I don't want to be forced
Into a life of continual crime
I can see for myself that the sun is sinking
How I wish you were here to see
Tell me now, am I wrong in thinking
That you have forgotten me?

Verse 6:
Now, they worry and they hurry and they fuss and they fret
They waste your nights and days
Them I will forget
But you I'll remember always
Old memories of you to me have clung
You've wounded me with words
Gonna have to strighten out your tongue
It's all true, everything you have heard
Chorus:

Verse 7:
In you, my friend, I find no blame
Wanna look in my eyes, please do
No one can ever claim
That I took up arms against you
All across the peaceful sacred fields
They will lay you low
They'll break your horns and slash you with steel
I say it so it must be so

Verse 8:
Now I'm down on my luck and I'm black and blue
Gonna give you another chance
I'm all alone and I'm expecting you
To lead me off in a cheerful dance
I got a brand new suit and a brand new wife
I can live on rice and beans
Some people never work a day in their life
Don't know what work even means
Chorus:

Thunder On The Mountain

Words & Music by Bob Dylan

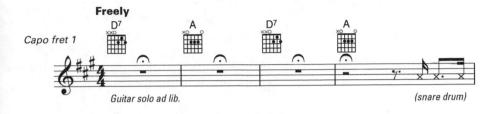

Freely

Capo fret 1

D⁷ A D⁷ A

Guitar solo ad lib. (snare drum)

Fast rock 'n' roll shuffle

1. Thun -

- der on the moun - tain, fires on the moon____ There's a

(Verses 4, 7 & 10 see block lyrics)

ruck - us in the al - ley and the sun will be here soon

To - day's the day, gon - na grab my____ trom - bone and blow____

Well, there's hot stuff here__ and it's
ev-e-ry where I__ go__ 2. I was think-in"bout A - li-
-cia Keys, could-n't keep from crying When she was born in Hell's Kit-chen, I was
(Verses 5, 8 & 11 see block lyrics)
liv - ing down the line I'm won- der- ing where__ in the world
A - li - cia Keys__ could be__
I been look- ing for her e - ven

clear through Ten-nes-see_____ 3. Feel__

___ like my soul is be - gin - ning to ex - pand look

(Verses 6, 9 & 12 see block lyrics)

in - to my heart and you will sort of un - der - stand__

You brought me here, now you're try-ing to run__ me a - way__

the writ -ing's on the wall, come

read it, come_ see what it_____ say__

291

Instrumental

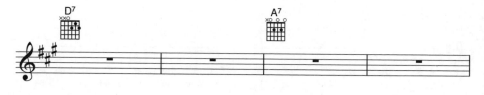

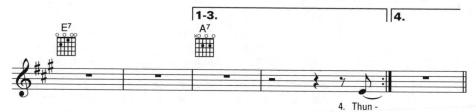

1-3.　　　　　　　　　　　　**4.**

4. Thun -

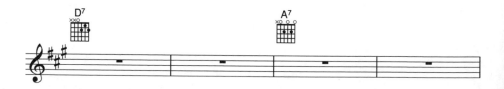

Instrumental cont.

Verse 4:
Thunder on the mountain, rolling like a drum
Gonna sleep over there, that's where the music coming from
I don't need any guide, I already know the way
Remember this, I'm your servant both night and day

Verse 5:
The pistols are poppin' and the power is down
I'd like to try somethin', but I'm so far from town
The sun keeps shinin' and the North Wind keeps picking up speed
Gonna forget about myself for a while, gonna go out and see what others need

Verse 6:
I've been sitting down studying the art of love
I think it will fit me like a glove
I want some real good woman to do just what I say
Everybody got to wonder what's the matter with this cruel world today

Verse 7:
Thunder on the mountain rolling to the ground
Gonna get up in the morning walk the hard road down
Some sweet day I'll stand beside my king
I wouldn't betray your love or any other thing

Verse 8:
Gonna raise me an army, some tough sons of bitches
I'll recruit my army from the orphanages
I been to St. Herman's Church and I've said my religious vows
I've sucked the milk out of a thousand cows

Verse 9:
I got the porkchops, she got the pie
She ain't no angel and neither am I
Shame on your greed, shame on your wicked schemes
I'll say this, I don't give a damn about your dreams

Verse 10:
Thunder on the mountain heavy as can be
Mean old twister bearing down on me
All the ladies of Washington all scrambling to get out of town
Looks like something bad gonna happen, better roll your airplane down

Verse 11:
Everybody's going and I want to go too
Don't wanna take a chance with somebody new
I did all I could and I did it right there and then
I've already confessed – no need to confess again

Verse 12:
Gonna make a lot of money, gonna go up north
I'll plant and I'll harvest what the earth brings forth
The hammer's on the table, the pitchfork's on the shelf
For the love of God, you ought to take pity on yourself

Someday Baby

Words & Music by Bob Dylan

Moderate shuffle

1. I don't care__ what you do,__
(Verses 2-13 see block lyrics)

I don't care__ what you say__   I don't care__ where you go__

__   or how long_____ you stay

Some-day__ ba - by,   you ain't gon-na wor-ry po' me__

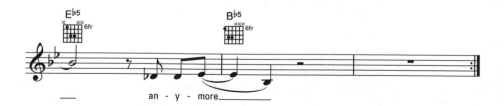

__   an - y - more_____

Verse 2:
Well you take my money and you turn me out
You fill me up with nothin' but self-doubt
Someday baby, you ain't gonna worry po' me anymore

Verse 3:
When I was young, driving was my crave
You drive me so hard, almost to the grave
Someday baby, you ain't gonna worry po' me anymore

Verse 4:
Instrumental

Verse 5:
I'm so hard pressed, my mind tied up in knots
I keep recycling the same old thoughts
Someday baby, you ain't gonna worry po' me anymore

Verse 6:
So many good things in life that I overlooked
I don't know what to do now, you got me so hooked
Someday baby, you ain't gonna worry po' me anymore

Verse 7:
Instrumental

Verse 8:
Well, I don't want to brag, but I'm gonna ring your neck
When all else fails I'll make it a matter of self-respect
Someday baby, you ain't gonna worry po' me anymore

Verse 9:
Instrumental

Verse 10:
You can take your clothes put 'm in a sack
You goin' down the road, baby and you can't come back
Someday baby, you ain't gonna worry po' me anymore

Verse 11:
I try to be friendly, I try to be kind
Now I'm gonna drive you from your home, just like I was driven from mine
Someday baby, you ain't gonna worry po' me anymore

Verse 12:
Living this way ain't a natural thing to do
Why was I born to love you?
Someday baby, you ain't gonna worry po' me anymore

Verse 13:
Instrumental (to fade)

When The Deal Goes Down

Words & Music by Bob Dylan

Moderate waltz

Capo fret 1

1. In the still of the night, in the world's an-cient light

(Verses 2-4 see block lyrics)

Where wis - dom grows up in strife

My be- -wil - der - ing brain, toils___ in vain

Through the dark-ness on the path-ways of life

Each in -

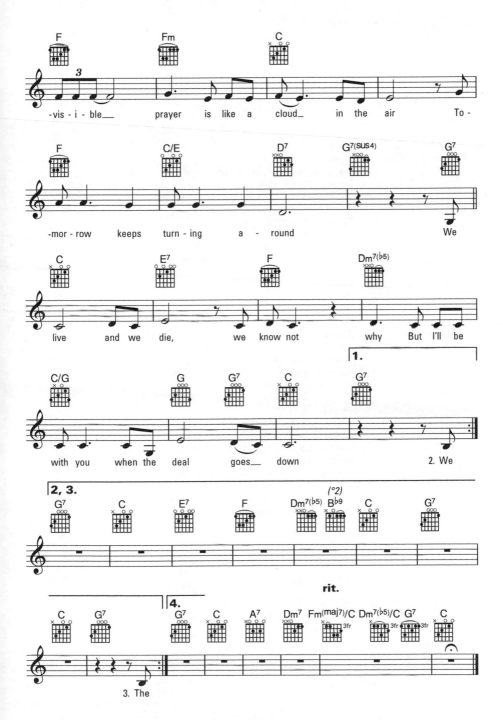

-vis - i - ble___ prayer is like a cloud___ in the air To-

-mor - row keeps turn - ing a - round We

live and we die, we know not why But I'll be

1.

with you when the deal goes___ down 2. We

2, 3.

(°2)

rit.

4.

3. The

Verse 2:

We eat and we drink, we feel and we think
Far down the street we stray
I laugh and I cry and I'm haunted by
Things I never meant nor wished to say
The midnight rain follows the train
We all wear the same thorny crown
Soul to soul, our shadows roll
And I'll be with you when the deal goes down

Verse 3:

The moon gives light and shines by night
I scarcely feel the glow
We learn to live and then we forgive
O'er the road we're bound to go
More frailer than the flowers, these precious hours
That keep us so tightly bound
You come to my eyes like a vision from the skies
And I'll be with you when the deal goes down

Verse 4:

I picked up a rose and it poked through my clothes
I followed the winding stream
I heard a deafening noise, I felt transient joys
I know they're not what they seem
In this earthly domain, full of disappointment and pain
You'll never see me frown
I owe my heart to you, and that's sayin' it true
And I'll be with you when the deal goes down

Life Is Hard

Music by Bob Dylan
Words by Bob Dylan & Robert Hunter

1. The eve-ning winds are still   I've lost the way and will

Can't tell you where they went   I just know what they meant

I'm al-ways on my guard_   Ad-mit-ting life is hard_   With-out you

near me   2. The friend you used to be   So near and dear to me

You slipped so far a-way   Where did we go a-stray   I pass the old school-yard_

299

Ad - mit - ting life is hard_ With - out you near me

Ev - er since the day___ The day you went a - way

I felt that emp - ti - ness so wide I don't know what's wrong or right I

just know I need strength to fight_ Strength to fight that world out - side

3. Since we've been out of touch I have - n't felt that much

From day to bar - ren day My heart stays locked a - way

I walk the boul - e - vard___ Ad - mit - ting life is hard___

With - out you near me 4. The sun is sink - ing low

I guess it's time to go I feel a chill - y breeze

In place of me - mo - ries My dreams are locked and barred___

Ad - mit - ting life is hard___ With - out you near me

With - out you near me_____

Beyond Here Lies Nothin'

Music by Bob Dylan
Words by Bob Dylan & Robert Hunter

Moderately fast

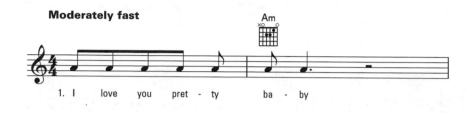

1. I love you pret - ty ba - by

You're the on - ly love I've ev - er known___

Just as long as you stay with me   the whole world is my

throne___   Be - yond here___ lies no - thin'

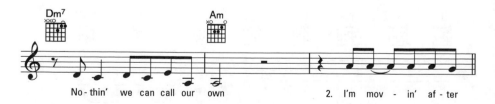

No - thin' we can call our own   2. I'm mov - in' af - ter

mid - night   Down bou - le - vards of bro - ken   cars

Dm⁷

Don't know what___ to do with - out it   With - out this love that we call

Am   E

ours   Be - yond here___ lies   no - thin'

Dm⁷   Am

No - thin' but the moon and stars   3. Down ev - 'ry street there's a

win - dow   And ev - 'ry win - dow made of   glass___

Dm⁷

We'll keep on lov - in' pret - ty   ba - by   For as long___ as love will

last___ Be - yond here___ lies no - thin' But the

moun - tains of___ the past___ 4. My ship___ is in the

har - bor And the sails___ are spread___

Lis - ten to me pret - ty ba - by Lay your hand___ up - on my

head___ Be - yond here___ lies no - thin'

No - thin' done___ and no - thin' said___

1 2 3 4 5 6 7 8 9

304